Praise for *An Orphan's Tale*

"This book shines a difficult light on what far too many orphans experience. I am grateful that this book brings awareness to the needs so many are facing and I'm convinced those who've never known this segment of our society can relate and choose to make a difference."

~ Tom Ziglar, CEO, Ziglar, Inc., proud son of Zig Ziglar

"Just reading the back cover… takes me back to the children I've worked with as a social worker. It reflects the pain, anger and strong will they have to survive.

This book helps the readers to understand their terror and their pain, from the beginning to the end.

It explains what kind of family is required… to make their new life a successful one.

Great job, Michael!"

~ Cheryl Trayler, LCSW

"With An Orphan's Tale: Hard Knox Chronicles, I became The Orphan as I flipped through the pages. I felt, hoped and even lived through his tragedies and adventures.

This book will change lives, as it has changed mine. Now more than ever, I understand how important it is to donate my time and resources back to the community that I live in."

~ Dwan Gant, Air Force Veteran, MBA

"The Orphan's story is one of tragedy and deep sorrow; yet his courage, perseverance and the ability to grapple with massive challenges is inspiring and triumphant.

A true tale of loss and teeth-gritting gain as he searches for belonging and finds himself within."

~ Suzanne Holman, Educator, Humanitarian and World Traveler

"WOW! I was done reading **An Orphan's Tale: Hard Knox Chronicles** *before I knew it. From one heart stopping scene to the next, this book keeps you engaged and runs out of pages too soon."*

~ Samantha Barns, Reading Enthusiast

"Reading **An Orphan's Tale: Hard Knox Chronicles** *made me feel like a fly on the wall in a world I didn't think could really exist in today's society. I am awake now and I am rooting for The Orphan and those like him. Can't wait to see what he does in the next book!"*

~ Carl Hemming Esq.

"When reading **An Orphan's Tale: Hard Knox Chronicles,** *be prepared to laugh, cry, hope and even hate for The Orphan. The stage is set and by the end of the book, you will be on Team Orphan!"*

~ Thomas Seehafer, Founder and CEO
of The Colorado Phoenix Project

"Be prepared to process a lot when reading **An Orphan's Tale.** *The author hits on subjects in graphic detail. It will force you into an emotional roller coaster. Intense. Powerful. Mind-Altering."*

~ Stefanie Savell, SHRM, Entrepreneur, Health and Wellness Mentor

"There was a trigger warning, but nothing could prepare me for what I read in **An Orphan's Tale: Hard Knox Chronicles.** *B. T Cox said he would point out some of the greatest and darkest attributes of humanity, and he delivered. I'm hooked and need to know what The General does to The Orphan as punishment in the next installment!"*

~ Emily Henderson, Survivor

*"***An Orphan's Tale: Hard Knox Chronicles** *offers a compelling and emotionally resonant portrayal of the American foster care system, seen through the eyes of a young orphan named Michael. Cox's poignant story deftly exposes the cognitive dissonance we are all guilty of as a society and the foster care system's failure to address its inherent problems and paradoxes. It is a must-read for anyone involved in adoption, social work, or leadership as it provides valuable insights from those who have experienced the system firsthand."*

~ Jay Martinez, Ed.D., Interdisciplinary Leadership

An Orphan's Tale:
Hard Knox Chronicles

A Novel
by
Bonar. T. Cox

Dedication

This book is dedicated to all six of my children and to those who dedicate their lives to the protection and education of the defenseless victims of foster care, trafficking, and family-less environments.

Due to the efforts of so many people in my own life, I was able to overcome the experiences of my humble beginnings. It takes a community to raise a child and without the recreational sport coaches and volunteers, teachers, public officials, and the loved ones in my life, I would not have been able to become the person I am today.

Together we can bring more awareness and resources to a root problem of so many societal issues. It all starts, and ends, with our youth. By focusing our resources on the next generation, we secure the next one.

Thank you to all the known and unknown influences in my life. *An Orphan's Tale* is written for you, and because of you.

Author's Note

Thank you for taking the time to read *An Orphan's Tale: Hard Knox Chronicles*. Each chapter has been carefully constructed to address some of society's greatest, and worst attributes. This is done through an orphan boy navigating his way through foster care and the adoption process. It will take a strong and understanding individual to not only read but absorb the emotional content within these pages.

This novel is written as fiction but will feel very real. There are some scenes in this book that could be triggers for you. If you have experienced any type of abuse, medical trauma or violence, please let a family member, friend or professional you trust know that you are reading this book. You may even consider having them read or discuss it with you. Whether you read it with someone else or if you are going to read it on your own, having a journal to jot down thoughts and feelings is suggested.

Although An Orphan's T*ale: Hard Knox Chronicles* may be hard to read, my hope it that it will be a beacon of hope to many. As individuals, we cannot control the lives we are born into, but we can control the destiny of our futures. The Orphan proves this through his experiences and gives others a roadmap to do the same. There are millions of orphans and foster children across the globe, just like The Orphan in this book. My goal is to bring awareness and resources to those who were unplanned, unwanted, and unaccounted for—just like I was.

"How much can you forgive?"

Dear Adult,

I had the memory beaten out of me, but now I see

I had a voice, but it was taken from me; no, not by choice, but by greed

The bruises were there, but you didn't care,

You saw the pain, as I watched you walk away

But I do not care about that, not now, no way

So could you please find mercy and love me, even for a day?

Signed,
The Orphan

1 The Social Center

"What the hell happened to my son? He has bruises over half of his body!" The Male Adult leaned forward, balancing on his toes, face red with anger and finger pointing aggressively at his "foe", which in this particular case happened to be The Social Worker.

Relief washed over The Orphan as he realized The Male Adult was mad at The Social Worker, and not at him. Not wanting to bring attention to himself, he looked out the building window, pretending not to be listening or to even understand what was going on. In fact, he understood exactly what was going on, and everything was fine as far as he was concerned. As long as everyone was mad and yelling at each other, they couldn't be mad and yelling at him.

"Mr. Tabernacky, you have seen Michael's file, so you know what he has gone through. There was no happy beginning for this boy and it's going to be up to you to provide a suitable ending to his childhood." The Social Worker spoke in a calm, practiced manner.

"That did not answer my question. The adoption papers were final three weeks ago. Why was he placed in other foster homes? You better hope my family practitioner doesn't find any serious damage because if he does, so help me God...."

The Social Worker cut him off before he could finish. "Mr. Tabernacky, foster care is tough on children and there are limited resources for everyone involved. Most of our foster parents are in it for the check, not the child, and the lines of corporal punishment are not clearly defined because they vary from home to home. We eliminate the foster homes where beating, molestation, and rape have been reported, but by the time we prove the charges, the damage has already been done. With several temporary foster homes in the last year, I am afraid Michael has been exposed to very little good in life so far. Michael is a difficult child, but a man of your accomplishments with a family as large as yours should be able to provide the atmosphere he needs to stabilize."

He folded his arms.

She continued, "If he becomes too much, remember that you can bring him back. Lord knows, plenty of foster parents have. Michael is used to being handed back, so try to minimize the damage and bring him back sooner rather than later. Personally, I don't think he will ever actually belong to a home, but I have the utmost confidence you can last longer than the others." She sounded almost as if she was trying to antagonize The Male Adult.

He took the bait.

"You make it sound as if he has no choice in the matter, that he should give up hope and fall in line with your boxed perception of what his future looks like. These are children, more importantly, human beings with the ability to CHOOSE the direction they take in life. The fact that he has been treated like an animal being passed from shelter to shelter makes me question what kind of systems our tax dollars support, especially programs that seem to systematically give up all hope and dreams for the future of those placed in their care." The Male Adult was determined to get his point across, but The Social Worker wasn't having any of it.

"Excuse me for my pessimism, Mr. Tabernacky, but it's hard to have hope when you know what has been done to him and what it has turned him into. Michael is not a normal child. He is very intelligent; he knows how to manipulate better than any adult I have met. When I first took his case, he was half dead in the hospital from malnutrition and blunt force trauma to the head. He almost died because his foster parents let his bronchitis turn into pneumonia, then beat him half to death for making a fuss about it. The next foster home used him as an ashtray. He had burn marks all over his body, and his hair always smelled like it had been singed. A year later when we thought all was well, Michael dropped his shorts and showed me his genitalia in hopes I would buy him a Coke. I have seen every foster care parent that has walked into his life promise the world only to watch them..." She trailed off, unable to find the words to continue.

She looked at The Orphan, and he ran to her without thinking. He knew he was never going to see her again, and he was about to say goodbye to the only person that had ever cared for him. She gave him a quick hug and walked away without saying goodbye, and without looking back.

He watched her walk away without a tear in his eyes. He didn't have any tears left for the people who walked out of his life.

The parents gently grabbed him by the shoulders in a reassuring way and walked him out of the community center. The Orphan was in a state of shock as the family guided him through the parking lot. Without a word, he climbed into their vehicle, sat where they pointed, and fell asleep before they even pulled out of it.

When The Orphan woke up, there was an invisible haze in the old Bronco II on the way to Bloomington from Albuquerque; more noticeable was the uncomfortable silence between the newly inte-grated family. The two girls were in the back with The Orphan. Both of them had a look of utter disgust and silent amusement on their faces while The Orphan had a look of embarrassment and mischief reflecting on his own.

It wasn't my fault that I had had pork and beans for lunch at the community center that I had called "home" for the past few hours, he thought begrudgingly, trying not to flush with embarrassment.

Finally, without warning, The Male Adult rolled down the windows and broke out into a laugh unlike anything The Orphan had ever heard. It was like he was forcing air out of his mouth and all that would come out was a wheezing sound, followed by a kind of muted coughing noise as his lungs ran out of breath.

He slapped his hand on his leg as he was driving and yelled, "Michael, you are rotten!" with a joking tone that brought a smile to the four-year-old's face.

That prompted the girls sitting on either side of The Orphan to break out into a fit of giggles and wayward glances. The Mother was all but hanging out the window, trying to gasp for fresh air to provide relief from the makeshift trap created by The Orphan's chronic flatulence.

It was at that moment that The Orphan realized this family was a little different than the others. They smiled for a start, wore nice clothes, and smelled clean. No fear was in The Sisters' eyes or voices and The Parents asked questions, listened, replied, and acted like they cared about what the girls had to say. Their body language was different, too. It was not aggressive or sexual. They seemed comfortable with their bodies, wearing tank tops and shorts; but, the most noticeable difference was that there were no bruises or marks on their bodies.

The Orphan liked them, he decided. He had to find out who they really were, of course, but on the outside they seemed like a television family, happy and perfect. He knew this wasn't how they really were, however. "The lessons of foster cares past" made sure he wasn't that naive. His mind started to wander as the scene continued to play out in front of him.

Unsettling memories of a not-so-distant time started to creep into his head as the voices and faces around him faded until he was in another world entirely. In a matter of minutes, he was asleep again, and in a nightmare-induced slumber.

 **Easter**

It was Easter Sunday, and there was an Easter basket sitting under a fake Christmas tree that had never been torn down and stored away. There was a single ornament with the face of the green Grinch painted on it. The Orphan hated the Grinch, with its wicked grin and evil eyes, but it went deeper than that. The Orphan had always been plagued with nightmares. When he woke up in the middle of the night, "it" would be there. Illuminated by the night light, The Orphan would stare at its crooked smile and slanted eyes, drifting in and out of slumber, not wanting to return to his nightmares, but not wanting to look at the Grinch's hungry stare when he opened his sleepy eyes.

Located just out of reach was an Easter basket filled with plastic eggs bursting with candy. He knew better than to reach for them. He would have to wait until he was given permission or until he earned it.

The Orphan was a pitiful sight with a mop of brown hair left uncombed, a body covered in dirt and filth, and ribs poking out of a hungry, bloated belly covered in black, purple and blue bruises. However, he looked healthy despite his neglect, with big round dimples penetrating green eyes and smooth, olive-colored skin.

He stared at the basket with those green eyes widened, more hungry than excited for the holiday. He wanted to eat so badly; he could feel saliva dripping down his chin. If there had been any witnesses to see it, the struggle was plain, a battle between primal survival and human morality. Finally, instinct took over. He crawled over to the basket, tipped it over and started eating the candy, not even taking the time to open the wrappers, chewing and swallowing the foil and plastic wrappings along with the sweet surprises inside. Flavor burst into his mouth as the jellybeans released their treasured flavors, chocolate ran like a river of mud—coating his throat, and the rich texture of caramel buried itself under his tongue. Nothing mattered but this gluttonous display of indulgence, but he knew instinctively that there was going to be a price to pay for this bad behavior. With a full belly and tired eyes, The Orphan drifted into a dreamless sleep.

Before The Orphan could even open his eyes, he could feel "it." His body temperature was hot and cold at the same time, the room he was in shrank and spun in circles making him dizzy, and his stomach knotted and churned as if some hidden monster had been awakened. His eyes snapped open as his heart started to thump uncontrollably. He started gasping for air as he broke out into a cold sweat. The panic was setting in. There was no hiding place, no sanctuary or hallowed ground to seek refuge. He was alone, he was defenseless, and if he was going to live, he was going to have to prepare himself mentally and physically.

The Orphan's mind raced. "Remember to be meek, but don't give in too soon. Stay beaten, but don't break until 'its' rage has passed its peak. Overreact at the point of contact to make the blows seem harder; and, most importantly, never ask 'it' to stop." With one long deep breath, The Orphan exhaled, closed his eyes, and waited.

The door opened.

"What the F**K! Michael, did you do this?! Look at what you did, you little shit!" The voice cracked like a whip.

The first blow knocked The Orphan's head against the drywall, putting a dent in it before being pulled off his feet and thrown back onto the ground where a pile of his dirty diapers lay. Something slammed into his exposed ribs; his breath was gone as his body went limp, and he lost consciousness.

When he opened his eyes, he was alone again—and "it" was gone. He was naked, battered, and bruised. In "its" rage, "it" had taken a curling iron and burned him, all over his body. His skin was on fire; moving from one side to the next only made the pain worse. He could feel the urine and feces on his burns, which made it seem like ants were biting him all over his body.

As he drifted off into a sobbing sleep, The Orphan considered himself lucky. He had been through worse, and he was alive. Then he allowed a tiny part of his deepest desire to hope he would find a family soon.

Like a shutter, his mind snapped to another lesson he had learned in foster care.

3 The "U" Driveway

Sarah was rich, he had heard.

"She has a big 'U' driveway you can ride your hot rod on, Mikey. This is going to be the one. I've heard she has so many toys for little boys, you won't know what to play with first. Plus she has fostered many orphaned kids, so she will treat you well." The look on The Social Worker's face had hope and sympathy on it as she described his new foster home. It would be the fourth foster home this month, and each had seemed worse than the last.

He had seen The Social Worker cry for him many times. She tried to explain what was happening, but he didn't understand her. She was careful with him, protected him, and got angry with him. She was even pretty, like the moms on TV with long, brown, curly hair, black penetrating eyes, and pale, white skin. He had even wanted to ask her if she would be his mom, but fearing rejection, never did. If he had a mom, though, he would have wanted her to be like The Social Worker.

When they pulled up to the house, The Orphan's jaw dropped. It was the biggest house he had ever seen! In that instant, he forgot he was an orphan, and he became a little boy again. The Social Worker was grinning from ear to ear as she heard her little Mikey talking about riding his hot rod tricycle, playing in sandboxes, and making new friends.

As he was shown to his room, The Orphan's doubts about The Social Worker's stories were put to rest as a smorgasbord of toys lay before him. His mind flooded with thoughts of all the adventures he would go on. His eyes were shimmering and his soul was singing as he turned and hugged The Social Worker before diving onto his new floor to start playing.

They were everywhere! He-Man and G.I. Joe action figures placed meticulously on the shelves. Tonka Trucks lay at the foot of the bed, ready for all the adventures and crashes they had been built for. Never before had The Orphan seen such a treasure; a playground to satisfy any desire he could conjure up.

"Play here while I take The Social Worker around the rest of the house, Michael," Sarah said in a pleasant and inviting tone.

"Sure!" The Orphan shot back with a huge grin.

Minutes flew by as The Orphan explored all the playtime options given. He was lost in the adventures of his imagination. He had not realized that The Social Worker had left, and Sarah was now watching him destroy her carefully laid-out room. If he had, he would have noticed her red ears, pursed lips, and squinted eyes; but he hadn't, so the attack blindsided him before he could set up his defenses.

"What the hell do you think you are doing? Those are not the toys that you are supposed to be playing with!" Sarah was seething with anger.

She had short, graying hair, wore thick bifocals, was slim, and seemed shorter than other adults. She did not look like a girl or a mom to The Orphan. She looked like a boy in a woman's body. She didn't wear girl or mom clothes either, and The Orphan had thought she looked a little masculine—and funny.

But he wasn't laughing now.

Several minutes passed, and The Orphan was balled up in the corner of the room, recovering from the flurry of slaps and closed-fist punches he had just absorbed from this new temp-parent. She was a lot stronger than she looked, and she knew what she was doing. She hit him in all the right places. A full body inspection would have to be done to see the kidney and groin shots, and the bare fisted blows his head had taken that his hair would conceal. Of course, a full body inspection would never happen because The Social Worker wouldn't suspect anything. When she would visit, The Orphan would be pretending to play neatly with the toys he was not supposed to play with. The Social Worker, not wanting to interrupt the only enjoyment she had seen him have, would leave him be, unquestioned. He could not cry out or beg for help, because if he did and The Social Worker did not listen, the beatings would become more severe.

He knew the drill, and he would play along. He had to.

It will get worse if she hears your cry.

The thought spun through his mind like a lifeline, repeating itself over and over as reality abruptly jolted him. He was still getting hit as the tears streamed down his cheeks, but he steadied his breathing and remembered how fun it had been to play with those He-Man figures and Tonka trucks. Someday, he would have all of them in a room where he could play all day without worry of retaliation.

The pain was gone and, at some point, the hitting stopped, but none of it mattered. He was in his own world now, one away from his body and the things adults did to it. While, physically, he was being pummeled, mentally, he was playing with toys, eating all kinds of food, and hugging people with no faces—with open arms. The pain was a distant memory as a dad worked with him outside, a mom kissed his boo-boos, and other kids played with him at the park.

At some point, he realized the hitting had stopped, and Sarah was talking to him.

"These were the toys you were supposed to play with," she scolded, rubbing her sore knuckles, and then opened a wooden chest at the foot of the bed with a soiled stuffed teddy bear and two Hot Wheels cars inside.

The Orphan did not even look up, refusing to let her see the pain on his face.

"The rules in this house are simple, and the consequences severe if you break those rules. As you can see, I have a quick temper, and even faster hands. It would be good for you to remember such things. The more rules you break, the harder your punishment will be. You will call me, 'Ma'am', and I am not your mother, so you better never refer to me in that fashion. You are here because neither your mother, nor anyone else for that matter, wanted you, so you will stay here as long as you're worth the pay."

The Orphan stared at the floor.

She continued, "I have read your file. You are a devilish child with no discipline or boundaries. It might have been better if you had not been born, but you were, and so here we are. I am here to tell you that your hell-raising days are over! I get paid to take care of you, so that means that this is a business transaction. Everything you do inside this house is treated that way. I make money from raising unwanted children, such as yourself, but I provide a place for you to stay and food to eat, and that is all you need and all you get. Do you understand?"

"Yes, Sarah," The Orphan replied meekly.

Slap!

The Orphan was hit across the face so hard, he could feel the imprint of her hand on the side of his cheek burning.

"You will refer to me as 'Ma'am.' Do you understand?! You will give me the proper respect for taking care of you when no one else would."

The Orphan couldn't find any words to speak.

Slap!

The other cheek was struck, as a ringing sound echoed throughout his head.

"I don't have time to sit here and decide if you are going to answer me or not! Do you understand?" She leaned over him, prepared to continue hitting him until she was satisfied with The Orphan's responses.

"YES, MA'AM!" The Orphan screamed, before she could rear back to deliver another blow.

"Do not hesitate; answer me promptly and respectfully." Her voice was flat, and her eyes bored holes into him. He could see hatred in those eyes. He had seen it many times and was used to its empty, cold gaze.

"Yes, Ma'am," The Orphan replied quickly and obediently, eyes averting to the shag carpet in his new room.

That memory faded into another.

 **The Room**

There was a hidden room. He didn't know how he knew it was hidden other than it was.

It had no windows, with a single bed. He couldn't move. He was pinned, gagged, and his skin was hot with a fever-like feeling, almost as if he were being pricked with a thousand needles at once. There were voices laughing, mocking, angry, and scary. Faces were dancing in front of him, each more unrecognizable than the next. There were others in the room like him; they were not on the bed, but he could see them in the corner, huddled and scared. Some had the look of frightened rabbits ready to bolt; others had the look of the living dead staring as if their souls had left long ago.

"It" was here.

The Orphan could sense "its" presence, "its" smell, "its" rot, and feel "its" hunger.

"It" was waiting. "It" was coming for him like a thief in the night, and he had to run, escape, and he had to...

WAKE-UP!!!

5 The Ride Home

Sitting in the Bronco, The Orphan jerked awake. Tears of pain were pouring down his cheeks, but more accurately, they were tears of a truth that would help shape the rest of his life. He was alone, and no matter who came into his life, for whatever amount of time, nothing was going to change that. He would never feel the connection or the bond of being a part of a group of people, and it was going to be up to him to make the best out of every situation and accept whatever life offered.

He realized that he had been sobbing out loud during his slumber, and the sisters were trying not to stare at him, now that he was awake.

"Why does he have bruises all over his body?" The Younger Sister to his right asked, interrupting his train of thought.

"Valerie! What did I tell you! You will not talk to him about his body, or his past, until your daddy and I say so!" The Mother admonished in a desperate but firm voice.

"It's okay; people ask me all the time," The Orphan replied, as if it was a normal question to be asking a toddler.

He looked at The Younger Sister and whispered, "'It' got me."

"Enough!" The Mother almost shrieked.

There was an awkward silence, which The Orphan took as his fault, so he laid his head on the back of the seat and drifted back to sleep.

When The Orphan woke up, he noticed an array of different colors dancing across his vision as he looked at the brilliant southwestern sunset. Mesmerized by the colors, a sense of peace settled inside of him. Purple, red, blue, orange, yellow, and pink, there were so many colors, all The Orphan could do was stare in amazement.

In the background, there was a rocky silhouette that resembled a gigantic ship sinking into the barren earth. It looked proud and defiant as it stood against the brilliant backdrop, almost as if it were fighting for its life, trying to prevent itself from being swallowed by the very earth that created it. This mountain became a symbol to The Orphan as time went on. Like the mountain, he was alone in a life-or-death struggle to not just survive, but rise above all others, to be noticed, and not be swallowed or defeated by the forces working against him. This mountain made him believe that it was okay to be alone, be different and, most importantly, it marked the start of a chapter he knew was going to be better than the rest that had come before it.

"Ugh. Why does he always have to fart in my direction?" The Sister said in a congested tone, due to her pinched-shut nostrils.

The Orphan looked to his right; the sister named Valerie had her arms crossed with a pouty look on her face. She was slender with dark skin and was all knees and elbows.

"How old are you?" The Orphan asked her, seeing an opportunity.

"Almost eight," she replied immediately.

The Orphan noticed that her tone was not judgmental, disgusted, or even condemning. It almost seemed as if she was actually interested in answering him.

"Well, I turn eight the same month you turn three," she corrected herself.

He could tell she was proud that she knew something about him.

It was at that moment he decided that he should let this family know that he liked them.

"How long are you going to keep me?" The Orphan asked with a steady voice.

Maybe it was the indifference of his tone or the matter-of-fact manner in which he presented the question, but sadness overcame the entire family.

The Orphan regretted the question immediately. He knew better than to ask adults questions. Adults hated to be bothered by children, especially children who were not theirs. He hoped he wouldn't get into trouble over this. A wave of fear swept over him as he realized he may have pushed too far.

"You will be here forever, Michael. We are never going to take you back. I am your Dad, this is your Mom, and those are your Sisters." The Adult Male's gaze was intense, almost challenging him to disagree, a challenge that The Orphan would normally meet gaze-for-gaze, if even for a moment, just to be defiant, but he relented, not wanting to interrupt.

The Orphan looked around. The Mother was crying, and The Sisters were looking down at the floorboard, as if ashamed of some unknown thing. It was a morbidly surreal moment that would permanently ingrain itself into the memory of The Orphan.

Deep down he knew it wasn't true because no one wanted him forever! He was willing to allow himself the pleasure of believing it for now, but he knew one day the reality of being an orphan would return to take him back to his personal place of solitude.

The sun had set by the time they pulled into the driveway at The House. The world seemed to stand still as he looked at all the newly built houses on quarter-acre lots. Young landscaping of a newly developed housing complex with an elementary school that was a stone's throw away gave the scene a suburban ambiance.

A blond girl who was riding her bike on the sidewalk looked up and flashed The Orphan a smile. He slowly walked to the edge of the driveway to watch her ride into the distance. She was beautiful. He had never seen a girl so beautiful, a neighborhood with so many houses, or a place where everything was so new. It was just like the TV shows he had always watched.

"You're cute!" the girl shouted as she turned around to make sure he heard her; then she peddled into the distance.

He had never seen such a pretty girl in real life, much less have one call him cute. He was blushing from ear to ear, wanting to say something back, but his limited vocabulary prevented the words from reaching his lips.

"Michael, come help carry stuff into the house," The Adult Male commanded, in a pleasant voice.

The Orphan paused for just a moment, hoping the pretty girl would turn around and come back his way. Feeling that he should hurry, or that The Adult Male might get angry, he turned around and bolted up the driveway with a single response.

"Coming, Dad!"

6 Buffy the Orphan Slayer

"Buffy doesn't like him that much!" the girl named Bridget exclaimed with a dubious face.

The Orphan had a look of shock, hesitation, and fear on his own.

The Dad was laughing uncontrollably, and The Mom knelt next to The Orphan with a look of concern on her face.

"Are you okay?" The Dad asked.

"Yes," The Orphan replied.

"Never look a dog in the eyes, son. A dog is loyal but, in the end, it's still its own master. When you invade their space or challenge their authority, they will defend what is theirs. In this case, that happens to be Buffy's pride and his dignity. Give him respect and he will be your best friend; disrespect him and his bark will turn into a bite."

The Orphan remembered the whole scene and replayed it in his head. He had heard of dogs before, but he had never actually seen one in person...

As he walked into the garage from the driveway, a fluffy cocker spaniel came rushing through the doggy door. He was awesome! Bouncing up and down in a fit of excitement to see its owners, standing on its hind legs with paws pawing for the attention it so desperately needed. Long floppy ears, a golden coat of fur, with the biggest tongue The Orphan had ever seen flopping from the side of its mouth, giving it a goofy appearance that made The Orphan let out a rare giggle.

He remembered running up to Buffy, stopping right in front of him, and bending over with a quizzical expression, examining it as a doctor would a patient.

Whack!

The Orphan felt something hard hit his forehead. When The Orphan opened his eyes, Buffy had retreated to some unknown place through the doggy door, barely missing The Dad's kicking foot on the way out.

The Orphan looked around to see what everyone else thought of his first lesson in animalistic behavior.

"What are you smiling at?" The Orphan asked The Sister named Valerie.

"You have two red bumps on your forehead! You look like you have two nipples growing above your eyebrows!" Valerie's eyes were squinting from the fit of giggling his appearance caused her.

"What are nipples?" The Orphan asked.

Bridget ran up to The Orphan and pinched him in the chest area. "These are nipples," she laughed, "and this is a titty twister!"

"Ouch!" The Orphan reeled back in fear of being pummeled.

Everyone was laughing so hard, they had tears in their eyes.

The titty twister didn't really hurt, but it took him off guard. All the physical contact he had ever had with anyone was painful and was connected to people being very angry with him. To have someone make body contact that was not abusive was something that he had to work through.

As he took in the scene around him, he also started to laugh. He was the butt of the joke again, not in a mocking or degrading way, but rather a warm and loving way. This was confusing but, nonetheless, it felt right, so he let himself enjoy the moment.

The Dad said they would keep him and not take him back, like all the other adults did.

No matter how bad he was, no matter what he did to make them angry, he was a "part of their family." That's what The Dad said.

He wanted to believe it, but he didn't. He would have to find a way to make them prove it!

The laughs faded away, and soon everyone was resuming their post trip duties. Somehow, he knew this "home" would be different than the rest.

7 Type 2 Diabetes

"There is something I must teach you, Michael." The Dad had a serious but controlled look on his face that snapped The Orphan's attention back to the moment at hand.

The Orphan instantly knew that play time was over. The Lady called "Ma'am" had taught him how to be serious.

The Dad took The Orphan into the house, guiding him by the back of the neck with one of his huge, calloused hands, through his newest home. Normally The Orphan would be tense with the invasion of his personal space, but the way The Dad rested his hand on his neck felt... well, it felt like a dad's hand, and that felt good.

Focused on the importance of the situation and not wanting to let his new dad down, he concentrated as they walked to a table that had open books and paper on it with pencils scattered all over the surface. Plants littered the kitchen and dining area as they walked through, giving the home a warm but unkempt look. Homemade arts, crafts, and baked goods littered the countertops and there was a sense of belonging that overcame The Orphan, almost as if he was "safe."

Dismissing the moment, not ready to trust his emotions, The Orphan brought himself back into reality as The Dad walked off into another room, after lifting his son up onto a chair close to the dinner table.

The Sister named Valerie was seated across from him. There was sadness on her face. She made eye contact with The Orphan, and there was a look of desperation there. He knew that look. It was the look of a person who felt as if they didn't belong, trapped in a world of "un-belongers." She was misplaced somehow and couldn't find where she fit in. She was sad too. She was good at hiding it, but he could feel the despair, depression, and hopelessness.

"I like you. Will you be my friend?" The Orphan asked, lighting up into the biggest smile he could muster.

"I am your sister. Of course I will be your friend!" she replied, almost dismissing the question.

"I don't want you to be my sister, just my friend. Okay?" The Orphan pressed; his smile was gone.

"Okay?" Valerie confirmed with hesitation, "Why though?"

"Can I tell you a secret?" The Orphan asked.

"Sure" she replied, looking to make sure no one was listening.

"Family always hurts me but friends are always nice to me. I know that you won't hurt me if you're my friend. If you're family, then well..." he let the sentence trail off, as if remembering things he wished forgotten.

The look in Valerie's eyes affirmed that he got his point across.

For most people, "family" meant safety and belonging, but for The Orphan, it meant pain and abandonment. Valerie must not have only seen it in her little brother's eyes, but she must have felt the urgency in his voice.

Valerie immediately brought her hand up to her mouth and spit on it.

She held it out to The Orphan. "Go ahead. Spit on your hand," she directed. "Once we shake hands, this agreement can't be broken. We will be friends, no matter what happens. Deal?"

She held her hand out for The Orphan to follow suit.

Without hesitation, he spit on his palm and shook her hand in return.

He knew she meant what she said. She needed him as much as he needed her, and they both seemed to recognize it. They stood there for a moment, hands held together.

Still caught up in the euphoric moment of making the first real social connections that either of them had ever had, The Dad's voice came bellowing from somewhere in the living room across the house.

"Okay, Valerie. It's time." His voice was carrying its usual unwavering tone.

She released her hand in a flash; the look of emptiness coming back onto her face. The Orphan tried to give her another confident smile, but it didn't work this time.

The Dad came over with a leather case in his hands.

"Your sister has a medical condition. She is sick and needs medicine every day. I am going to show you how to do this until you can do it yourself. The condition she has is called diabetes."

"This is a blood sugar monitor." He opened the leather pouch and took out a box-looking thing. "This is going to tell us what her blood sugar level is. If her blood sugar is too high or too low, it could really hurt her. Okay?"

"Okay," The Orphan agreed, just to agree.

"This is the tool we use to take her blood." He pulled out a pen-looking contraption.

"Inside it, there is a needle that is going to poke a hole in her finger. There will be blood, and it's okay because that blood helps us keep her healthy."

He handed the pen to The Orphan. "I want you to push this button when I tell you. Okay?"

The Orphan panicked.

"No!! I won't do it!!" he screamed. He tried to run, but The Dad caught him by the arm before he could make his retreat.

"Michael, I know you're scared, but you have to learn to do this. Valerie's life may depend on it someday, and I—and she—need to count on you. The Dad's voice was not threatening or impatient, but it was firm.

The Orphan stood there trying to decide if he should kick The Dad in the knee and run so he didn't have to do it. The Dad walked with a limp so it would have to hurt and, surely, he was fast enough to get away and find a hiding spot to let The Dad's anger pass.

He might get a beating, but at least Valerie would know he was on her side.

"Dad's right," Valerie pleaded, interrupting the heroic exit strategy that was building up in his imagination. "Please learn how to do it. I might need your help someday. Think of it. Mike the hero! Kinda has a good ring to it. Don't you think?" She flashed an amazing smile, and his defenses crumbled.

He stopped resisting. His body went almost limp with defeat as thoughts of his kick-and-run disappeared.

For the first time, he had a real friend. Not the kind you play with for a few hours at the community center, then never see again, but the kind that could last, and now he was going to have to hurt her.

Valerie held her finger out to The Orphan.

The Dad placed the pin on her finger. "Okay, Michael, go ahead," he encouraged in a calm voice.

The Orphan stood there, tears streaming down his cheeks.

"I'm sorry," he whispered to Valerie.

Snap! The pen clicked.

There was a jerk from Valerie, her eyelids snapping shut as the needle penetrated her skin. The Dad pushed on her finger where the needle went in to make the blood come out faster and, at the same time, pulled out a tiny strip of paper and placed the drop of blood on the tip of it. Satisfied with the blood placement on the strip of paper, The Dad carefully inserted it into the box.

"Watch the screen, Michael," The Dad instructed.

A number popped up on the screen.

"What does it say?" The Orphan asked.

"Well, her blood sugar is too high, Michael. That means we have to give her a shot and get some food in her so it can come down to the normal level."

"What's a shot?" The Orphan asked.

"It's a pain in the ass!" Valerie exclaimed, with a mocking smile on her face.

"Watch your language," The Dad warned, not as a command but more of a suggestion.

"Well, it is!" she cried out as she rolled her eyes.

Valerie turned around and pulled down her pants, leaving her butt exposed.

Embarrassment rushed through The Orphan as he turned away in shame. The house started to spin, his knees buckled, and sweat started to break out from pores all over his body. Things around him became blurry and sounds were fading in and out.

Then he passed out.

8 The Secret

When he awoke, he was not in the living or the dream world. He was in between.

Trapped inside a memory that did not welcome him but would not allow him to escape.

"You can't hide from me. You can't run from me. I am everywhere and nowhere. I will be here til the end of your time. I will be here til the end of all time. I will see you soon."

The voice was constant, taunting and torturing, making it impossible to find any kind of peace or refuge from its constant physiological bombardment.

"Michael. Michael." Another voice redirected his attention. It was The Social Worker. Hope sprung up inside, giving him renewed energy. She came back to save him, take him away from this place, and she would raise him like her own son! The thought quickly faded as he noticed the tone her voice carried.

"Michael. Remember our secret? You promised Michael, and you never break a promise. Don't tell anyone what happened because, if you do, no one will want you. You must always remember to keep this to yourself. Forever!" **Her voice was desperate, pleading, as if life depended on it.**

"His life." The thought came unabated.

9 Truth and Consequences

When The Orphan came to, The Dad was standing over him, looking down at him. Valerie was beside him, caressing his hair, and Bridget was staring at him as if she had seen a ghost.

"Don't call the ambulance. He will come around in a moment." There was confidence in the voice that was speaking. A confidence that he had only heard from one person in his lifetime.

It was The Dad.

"Why did he pass out, Dad?" It was Bridget asking the question. She must have come downstairs upon hearing all the commotion.

The Dad did not answer the question.

"Girls... I want you to start reading the new Bible book I got you to your brother every night. Start from the beginning like your mother and I did with you," The Dad suggested in a firm tone.

"The one with all the pictures and stories?" Valerie entered into the conversation.

"Yes, that's the one. I think it's time for Michael to learn who his Father is." There was determination in his voice but directed toward what, The Orphan could not tell.

The Dad was trying to protect him from something, but what does a book protect him from and how will it teach him who his father is?

Wait! He had a Father...?

The words burned themselves into The Orphan's soul.

The Orphan realized where he was and opened his eyes to see everyone looking down at him. Immediately, embarrassment turned into tears.

He ran to The Mom and buried his face into her chest, sobbing uncontrollably as she wrapped her arms around him and held him as close as she could.

Like The Dad's hand on the back of his neck, The Mom's embrace was different than the other moms. It was tight, warm, strong, unyielding and, for the first time in his memory, The Orphan felt what it was like to be embraced by a real mother.

Once The Orphan stopped crying and relaxed, The Dad walked over to where he was and knelt down so he was eye level with The Orphan.

"Did you know what part of the body that was Michael?" The Dad asked.

The Orphan slowly nodded his head yes.

"Why are you embarrassed? Did someone hurt you?" The Dad pressed.

The Orphan was looking at the floor now. He just shrugged his shoulders, not wanting to speak and not wanting anyone to see into his eyes. He knew what they would see, and he couldn't let that happen. He had a promise to keep.

He steadied himself and forced his mind in another direction, any other direction.

Satisfied that he could look The Dad in the eye again without spilling the beans, The Orphan slowly lifted his gaze to meet The Dad's.

Shock shot through The Orphan like a wave of adrenaline.

He knew! The Orphan could see it on The Dad's face. He would never know the details, but the dots had been connected and, for the first time, he saw uncertainty wash over his new father's face.

He looked around to see who else was paying attention. Bridget seemed uninterested; The Mom was still holding him close to her chest, chin resting on the mop of hair on the top of her son's head.

It was Valerie who caught his attention.

Her gaze was ripping into him. She knew as well! But how?

She was not embarrassed or grossed out like other kids but seemed... curious. She wanted to know more, and that meant breaking the promise. If The Social Worker was right, that meant that The Dad and Mom would take him back.

He felt helpless and, to make it worse, he didn't see any way out of it. He would do anything Valerie asked, even if it meant going back to the community center.

"Okay, Michael," The Dad acquiesced, gaining The Orphan's full attention once again.

"This is not a dirty thing. One day you might have to do this, so I need you to watch." The Dad's voice directed his attention to a needle being pressed into a glass vial, turned upside down, and filled with a clear liquid.

The Dad pulled the needle out, examined the measurement, and started to flick it.

"If you don't get the air bubbles out, they will enter into the bloodstream—and it could kill her, so you must make sure that you get all the air bubbles out. It's a matter of life and death. Do you understand?" The Dad didn't wait for an answer, confident that his point was a sufficient enough answer.

Valerie lazily leaned over, exposed the upper cheek of her backside, careful not to expose her whole buttocks this time, and braced for the needle to break her skin.

Satisfied that all the air bubbles had been expelled, The Dad took the needle and quickly poked it into her butt cheek after swiping the exposed skin with a potent-smelling piece of wet cloth.

"This has something called insulin in it that needs to be injected into her bloodstream. It brings her blood sugar back down. This is the medicine that saves her life, son." The Dad was dead serious.

The Orphan nodded as Valerie pulled her pants back up.

"I am going to ask you to do this someday. When I'm not around, you're the man of the house, and it's up to you to protect your mom and sisters. Can you do that, son?" The Dad had a pleasant tone. One that not only inspired him but actually made him believe that he was capable of doing what was being asked.

The Orphan nodded, trying to hide the disbelief that he was being trusted with such a responsibility.

"See. I told you it was a pain in the ASS!" Valerie yelled as she darted through the kitchen before The Dad could grab her. She ran up a flight of stairs, laughing.

The Orphan looked at The Dad, fearful that her disobedience would be taken out on him.

Instead, he saw a warm smile on The Dad's face. He was watching his disobedient daughter run away, and he wasn't angry at all.

He was amused!

What a confusing family! The Orphan thought.

"She is a strong little girl, Michael. Learn from her, because both of you are unique in your own special way." Sadness came over The Dad as he looked back down at The Orphan.

"It's not fair that you and your sister should have to deal with so much. Over all else, Michael, life's anything but fair, but you must focus on the things you can control, not the things you can't."

The Orphan soon realized that The Dad was reminding himself of this lesson as much as he was teaching his new son.

 A Boy Apart

"It's time for dinner." The Mom's voice rang out just as The Orphan thought how hungry he was from the trip to his new home from the community center.

The Orphan walked to the far side of the dining room, found a corner that did not have any plants cluttering it, pulled a chair over to it, and sat facing the windows that looked out into the backyard. His back was to the rest of the house, so he was oblivious to what was going on behind him.

Out there he marveled at the big backyard with a tall brown picket fence at the back end of the property. To the right was some huge contraption The Orphan couldn't even begin to piece together but he could make out a play set in the back corner of the yard, a sandbox under some upside-down giant bowl-looking thing, and a whole bunch of plants growing neatly in unilateral rows.

"Michael, it's time for dinner." Valerie was standing beside him, giving him a warm smile, motioning suggestively toward the dinner table and an empty spot at it.

The Orphan just looked at her, face blank, confused as to what she wanted.

She couldn't possibly be suggesting that I sit at the dinner table with them?!

The dinner table was a place for adults and family, not estranged children. This had always been the case, and he could not remember eating with a single family he had been fostered with. Even The Social Worker had encouraged him to eat in a separate area away from the adoptive family members.

The Social Worker's instructions came marching into his brain from some forgotten place.

"You must remember that they are your caretakers, not your parents. You are different, Michael. You are not their real son, and you need to let them keep their family identity separate while they include you into their life as they see fit. Even simple gestures such as inviting you to eat with them, join their conversations, or play board games could be nothing more than a test to see if you fit into their family. It's best not to participate or include yourself into anything that could show them an emotional side of you that they don't think will fit into their family structure or approval."

The Orphan was just standing there in indecision as The Mom's voice came ringing from the dining area.

"Valerie, come to the dinner table. It's time to eat," The Mom demanded.

"I'm not going to just let him sit here by himself, Mom. He is a part of the family, and he should be allowed to eat with us."

"I don't want to eat at the table. I want to eat here by myself," The Orphan's voice butted in, as he looked Valerie in the eyes, letting her know it was HIS choice.

"Michael, don't be mad. Look, we even set a place at the table for you. See!" Valerie's face was desperate as she pointed as "his" apparent seat at the table. She felt personally responsible for this alienation for some reason, and she was trying to make it right, any way she could.

"Valerie, now!" The Dad's voice shot in.

Valerie sighed, turned around, and made the short trip to her seat at the table.

The Mom brought a plate over to The Orphan and knelt in front of him, sitting it on his lap with a glass of water set carefully to the side. As she knelt to hand it to him, he could feel her hand on the small of his back, rubbing it reassuringly.

"Here is your dinner, honey," she urged with a proud smile.

"You are welcome to sit with us at the table. The social worker told us how you prefer to eat by yourself, but you are a part of our family, so you can join us whenever you want." The Mom's gaze was intent and almost assuming.

"Would you like to join us tonight?" Hope was in her voice.

"No." The Orphan responded immediately. Just as instant was the regret that followed.

The pain in The Mom's eyes was undeniable, and for a moment he almost caved and told her he would join them at the table, but he held firm.

Satisfied he wasn't going to change his mind, The Mom gave the worst fake smile he had ever seen, scratched his back for just a moment longer, and then went to her seat at the table to join the rest of the family.

The Orphan watched them grab hands as The Dad started to speak, but he could not understand what was being said. It sounded like the same language, but for some reason, he couldn't understand the words. They did mention the name Grace before he started to talk. Maybe it was a daughter of theirs who wasn't around or maybe even dead.

Once he saw everyone in the family take their first bite of food, he started to poke at what was set in front of him, not knowing exactly what it was.

It was some sort of meat that looked like a slice of bread and, for a lack of a better comparison, it looked as if there were a layer of blood on the top of it. It smelled good with the scent of onion and other unknown spices traveling up his nostrils, teasing his senses.

The Orphan patiently waited until everyone but himself started eating, and as soon as he saw that everyone had taken a bite, he figured that meant he could too.

All it took was the first taste, and he started to tear through the loaf of meat, ignoring the asparagus stems and applesauce beside it.

"Wow! I guess he likes meat." It was Bridget.

The Orphan could not see her, but he could feel her watching him.

"It's not polite to stare," The Mom chided her eldest daughter.

"Sorry, can't help it. He is amusing to watch," Bridget replied with what had to be a big grin on her face, judging from the enthusiasm in her voice.

The Orphan took it as a compliment and, as much as he liked Valerie, Bridget seemed to be the nicer and calmer of his two siblings.

The Mom brought over another slice of the meat and set it on his plate.

"Eat your vegetables," The Mom encouraged as she walked away with the pan holding all the food on it.

The Orphan started to pay attention to the dinner table, and everyone seated at it through the reflection in the window.

One by one, the family finished their meal. Bridget and Valerie asked permission to be excused from the table, cleared their dishes, and went to their room, which left The Orphan seated there by himself.

In no time, everyone was busy with their normal nightly activities.

Satisfied that no one was the wiser, The Orphan took some of the meat off his plate and stuffed it into his pockets.

This wouldn't be the first time a home tried to trick him with a nice meal and warm smiles just to hold food and water hostage later to get him to do and say the things they wanted in exchange.

He would find a hiding place in his new room and put the food there, just in case this family tried to do the same thing.

Satisfied that his pockets had enough food in them for a snack later, The Orphan asked to be excused.

The Dad came over, inspected his plate, obviously not approving of the uneaten asparagus and applesauce, but kept it to himself and granted The Orphan permission to be excused.

After The Mom washed his hands and face, complaining about what a messy eater he was, The Orphan breathed a sigh of relief as he realized that she had not noticed the food stuffed into his pockets.

Content that he was clean enough to go to bed for the night, she grabbed his little hand and walked him up the stairs into his new room.

He was forced to temper his enthusiasm for fear of making the same mistake as he did with the Ma'am lady, Sarah.

It was better than Ma'am's room, however! Not as big but it was painted a baby blue with art stenciled all over the walls. There was an actual bed, instead of just a mattress on the floor, a toy chest, a nightstand with a night light turned on, and a pair of pajamas laying on the neatly made bed for him to put on.

"Let your sisters know when you are done changing, son, and they will come in and read you a bedtime story," The Mom assured him as she closed the bedroom door behind her on the way out.

A smile was on The Mom's face, letting The Orphan know that he had failed in hiding his excitement.

She knew he loved his new room. The difference with her versus the other moms was... she seemed to be happy for him.

As soon as the door was closed, The Orphan went about the business of finding a suitable hiding place for his food stash. It wouldn't be hard to find food in this house, but he was going to have to find a big enough place to hide it all. His closet was small and cramped, making it the perfect spot to hide things. He reached into his pocket and pulled out the meat, placing it into a pair of hotrod underwear that was neatly folded in a pile of new clean clothes beside the closet.

Satisfied that he had wrapped the meat sufficiently enough to make sure it couldn't drop out of the makeshift container, he carefully placed it in the left hand corner of the closet under the lowest hanging shelf. He wiped his hands off on his pants, undressed, and put on his pajamas before walking to the door to get Valerie and Bridget.

When he opened the door, his sisters were already sitting right outside his room waiting for him.

Seeing the door open, they jumped to their feet and barged in.

"It's so good to have a brother! We are going to do so many fun things together, and we have so much to tell you, I don't even know where to start. I mean you have to make up for eight years with me and almost thirteen with Bridget! I don't know if we have enough time!" Valerie exclaimed.

"Calm Down! You are going to scare him to death!" Bridget interjected.

"Dad told us to read him a story and that was it for tonight. Remember that I am in charge until they come up to tuck him in, so you better do what I say." Bridget was giving Valerie a judgmental look with a tone to match.

"Ya. Whatever. Only because you are older," Valerie acquiesced solemnly.

"I get to read to him first!" Valerie lunged for the book before her sister could get to it.

She opened the book and started to read before Bridget could protest.

The Orphan listened as Valerie struggled to pronounce words and put sentences together. The book talked about how the world was made, how people were made, and how the creator named "The Father" did it all for His children, which happened to be all the people in the world.

Soon Bridget took over. She was a much better reader than Valerie was, and the words seemed to flow out of her mouth in a poetic form. The Orphan lost his train of thought and became lost in the world his older sisters had created for him through the book they were reading to him.

There was a baby that was placed in a river and saved by a king, a story he could relate to. There was a sheep herder who was put in charge of leading His people away from a bad place, after a burning bush told him to. That man's job was to protect the chosen people and lead them to safety after parting the ocean in half. The best story of all was how the ordinary man became famous by slaying a real giant named Goliath.

Slowly, The Orphan drifted off into a dreamless sleep. He really didn't know what all those things meant, but he did have a single passing thought before he drifted off to sleep.

I have a Father, and he made us ALL.

 Tunnel Vision

"Michael! Put that down or I will tell Dad what you were looking at!"

The Orphan was seated on the floor of his parent's room in the lower level of the three-story house. The Mom and Dad's waterbed and bedframe took up most of the room's space, giving it a more cluttered than elegant look. It was neatly made with pillows and extra blankets laid out in an almost artistic fashion. There were mirror panels that hung on the outside of the sliding closet doors and an old twelve-inch television clumsily placed on a bookshelf that was littered with loose books and folders.

It had been a couple of years since his adoption and in a routine canvas of all the places he was not supposed to be, The Orphan came across a drawer of The Dad's that had magazines stored in it. It was these magazines that had The Sister Bridget in an uproar.

There were no words to describe the look on Bridget's face as he looked up from the magazine and saw her expression. There was a mixture of shock and disgust on her face, coupled with a tinge of fear.

Noticing the indecision on her face, The Orphan decided to go on the offensive.

"Why? What's wrong with it? And why don't you look like that with your clothes off?" The Orphan asked, as innocently as possible without coming across as insincere.

Bridget looked like she had been slapped across the face by the question.

"Well, I am not grown up yet!" she finally managed, obviously at a loss for words. Her face contorted in a mixture of rage and frustration.

With that, she raised her chin, straightened her shoulders, and marched over to The Orphan, grabbing the "1986 Playboy Playmate Of The Year" magazine issue and throwing it back into their dad's open underwear drawer, where it had come from.

"Besides this is totally degrading to women and Dad shouldn't have these kinds of things in the house. I mean, he has daughters and a wife! Think of how this makes all of us feel. Dad is married and he looks at all these other women. It's disgusting, and it's not fair to all the girls who don't look like this. Should all of us be judged on looks, how skinny we are, and whether we look good without makeup or clothes? I think not!"

She went on and on about women's rights and the way men were treated differently in society when it came to sex, jobs, and overall equality.

All The Orphan could think of was the girl in that magazine and the way he felt when he looked at her. She was beautiful, but not in the way The Mom was, or even how he looked at The Sisters. She was something else entirely!

"If I were Mom, I wouldn't let him have them!" Bridget was pacing in front of The Orphan, now shaking her head from side to side in dissatisfaction.

"I don't know why, but I kinda like them," The Orphan sounded off unexpectedly, unintentionally interrupting her feminist tirade.

She stopped her pacing and just stared at him in utter disbelief.

"Michael, listen to me. I don't want you to look at these. Women shouldn't be objectified like this. Do you understand me?" She walked up in front of him, and her hands gripped his shoulders, as if it would help get her point across.

"What's 'objectified?'" The Orphan asked, breaking the intensity of the moment Bridget was trying to create.

"UGHHH! You're impossible! I think a rock would have been a better investment for Mom and Dad!"

She rolled her eyes, released her grip, and started to walk away.

"What's an 'investment?'" The Orphan prodded with a smile, knowing the additional question would send her over the edge.

He couldn't help but chuckle as she walked away, throwing her hands up in the air in disgust, giving up on trying to get through to her little brother.

Bridget was a smart person, and one thing he had learned about smart people was they expected you to be almost just as smart as they were. If not, they became quickly irritated and would end the conversation, not wanting to waste any more time.

The Orphan used this knowledge many times to end conversations he didn't want to have, and it worked with uncanny precision with Bridget.

"If Dad ever catches you looking at these, you are dead! DEAD, Michael! Stay out of here!" she yelled as she walked out of the room, not even bothering to look back to see if her warning had been heeded.

The Orphan watched her walk away. He was confused why looking at people without clothes was bad. He took a bath without clothes, and The Mom, Dad, and even The Sisters had seen him naked. Bridget hadn't gotten angry then. He had seen other kids and adults naked, and besides, if The Dad looked at girls in magazines and liked it, why was it bad for him to look at them and like it?

He didn't know the answer, but one thing he did know was he was going to have to be careful not to let anyone catch him next time he came to look at those pictures. There were so many magazines in there, he couldn't wait to see them all, and see them all he would.

The Orphan closed the underwear drawer where he had found the magazine and left the room to go watch his favorite movie, *The Ewoks*. The Dad would be home soon, and he had promised The Orphan they would go swimming when he got back.

 Sink or Swim

A few hours later, The Dad returned, and as promised, he bellowed out in his usual commanding voice that, "If we were going to go swimming, we had better be ready in five minutes."

It took less than that for The Orphan and The Sisters to slide into their bathing suits and dive into the pool.

The Orphan waited until The Mom had left to take her post-swimming shower and The Sisters were playing what was left of the game "Marco Polo" to ask The Dad a question that had been nagging him over and over in his mind since the incident with Bridget earlier that day.

"Dad?" The Orphan asked in the swimming pool, with floaties attached to each arm as The Sisters were getting out of the pool, bored with the game that everyone else had already quit playing with them.

"Yes, son." The Dad was waist deep in the pool, floating leisurely as The Orphan struggled to get his breaststroke technique to The Dad's standards.

"Is it okay to look at girls naked? I mean, if a girl wanted to take off her clothes for me, would I get into trouble?" The Orphan had been building up the courage to ask this question since Bridget had scolded him earlier that day.

The Dad broke out into an obnoxious laugh.

"Why, son? Are the girls knocking down your bedroom door? Have you become the neighborhood playboy before you've hit seven? Lock up your wives and daughters! Michael is on the prowl." There was a smile on his face, but definite sarcasm in his voice.

"I think I like the way girls look without clothes. Bridget says that it makes me a 'bad example of the male gender,' whatever that means." The Orphan was ignoring the sarcasm coming from The Dad.

He knew The Dad would eventually find out or catch him looking at those magazines, so he needed to know how much trouble he was going to get in.

"I think you're a little young to be looking at any girls naked. Don't you think so?" he asked seriously.

"But if it's not okay, why do so many people do it?" The Orphan was so sincere, it caught The Dad off guard.

The Orphan liked talking to The Dad. He always had the answer to everything and knew how to fix anything.

As his dad tried to formulate the correct answer, The Orphan's mind started to wander off into some of the things he had learned about The Dad over the past few years.

In the last few years with this family, The Orphan had learned that The Dad had been a war hero in a war called Vietnam, flew several tours as a helicopter pilot, killed lots of those assholes called "Charlie", and he was able to save the life of his co-pilot when his helicopter was shot down during his last mission.

One day, The Orphan asked him what it felt like to be a hero and all he said was:

"Son, real heroes never ask to be a hero, but when the time comes, they either respond or react. In Ranger school, they trained us to respond and adapt to any situation, and to overcome that situation or die trying. When the time came, I responded. I beat the odds. I survived, and I was given a hero's medal, but we were welcomed back as traitors when I came home. My own nation spit on my face, and dog shit was thrown on the uniform with those shiny medals my government was so proud to give me. So when someone says I am a hero, I say, 'I am a man that served my country, paid my dues, and earned the right to be called an American. I am nothing more, nothing less, and you keep your medals and your titles but, by God, let me live in peace.'"

The Dad's voice always trailed off when he talked of the war. When The Orphan asked why, The Dad would merely say, "War has a way of changing a man, son."

The Orphan was just holding onto the side of the pool's edge, patiently waiting for The Dad to answer.

Even in the pool, where you could see his big hairy belly and scars from his time of service, he was larger than life to The Orphan.

Whenever The Orphan got to spend time together with The Dad, he would pay attention to everything he said and did, from how hard he worked out in the yard to how he reasoned through complex problems.

The stories of his life were steppingstones to building how The Orphan wanted to view bravery, honor, and loyalty. He even paid close attention to The Dad's physical appearance, from how much hair was on his chest to how big his arms and forearms were, the grip of his hands, and his lifting power.

How a man that had such a fat belly could move so fast still amazed him. And just how in the hell does a man with two artificial knees out-sprint and out-distance run a six-year-old boy?

It was safe to say that, for The Orphan, The Dad was the perfect example of what a man should be.

The scars from his gunshot wounds, bayoneted stabbings, and surgeries showed The Orphan how tough and resilient a man's body should be. The way The Dad protected, provided for, and respected The Mom and The Sisters showed him how a man should love and treat a woman. The way he was patient with life showed The Orphan how to respect God's direction, and for him to submit his life to His will.

It was safe to say that the biggest hero in The Orphans life, rightfully so, was The Dad, and he wanted to be just like him.

The Dad's voice interrupted The Orphan's train of thought.

"Well, son, a woman is a precious thing, and in my opinion, the most precious thing the world has to offer. You have to treat them with respect. Never lose your temper, make fun of their bodies, or hit them, under any circumstances. It's natural for you to want to look at naked girls, although it usually happens a little later in life for most boys. God made the woman's body for man to enjoy, and He made the man's body for woman to enjoy, but we are commanded to do so within the confines of marriage. It is not a dirty thing, son, but it is not a thing that you need to be concerned with at this point.

"With that being said," he instructed firmly, "it's most certainly not okay for you to look at any girl naked or allow a girl to show you her body at any time. If it does happen, both of you will get in a lot of trouble."

He was trying to have a closed-ended conversation, taking his six years of age into consideration, but The Orphan was being very persistent.

"Why are my parts different from their parts?" The Orphan asked, eyebrows furrowed again.

The Dad chuckled.

"You stay away from their parts, son, and when it comes to your parts, I am only going to give you one piece of advice." The Dad lowered his voice, as if he were getting ready to share a secret.

"What's that?" The Orphan paddled closer so he could hear.

The Dad always gave good advice, but he hated repeating himself.

"Keep your pecker in your pocket." He said it as seriously as if he were sounding off one of the Ten Commandments.

"Keep my pecker in my pocket?!" The Orphan repeated, confused.

The Orphan thought about it. He knew what a pecker was. The Dad used that word exclusively for penis, but what he didn't understand was how to keep it in his pocket.

He could cut a hole in his jeans, but surely that would make The Mom mad. And it wasn't long enough to come out of the pants into the pocket, and even the thought of trying it seemed painful.

This didn't seem like good advice at all!

"All I am saying is, keep it out of places it doesn't belong," The Dad attempted to clarify and respond to the confusion on his face, obviously uncomfortable with the topic.

"Where does it belong?" The Orphan asked, even more confused.

"SHIT," The Dad cursed under his breath.

He jumped toward The Orphan, sending waves of water that raised up like a tsunami, ready to engulf whatever was in its path. Then The Dad picked up The Orphan and threw him across the pool.

He popped up out of the water in a fit of giggles, begging The Dad to do it again.

Instantly, The Orphan forgot about everything he and The Dad were just talking about and remembered the first summer with this family, and how they had taught him to swim.

What an amazing day that was!

Water made his skin feel new and clean. Almost as if all the filth and sin of his life were being washed away. He found he could control his OWN life, simply by dunking underwater while he held his breath and coming back up for air when his heart started to beat really hard.

Of course, he had not always felt this way.

He was terrified the first time The Dad put the floaties on his arms, picked him up, and yelled the words, "When your feet hit the bottom, make sure you kick yourself up; and don't forget to breathe when you break the surface." With no further instruction, The Orphan was tossed into the pool to sink or swim.

When The Orphan came up for air, it felt like he had been born again. With a nose full of water and eyes burning from the chlorine, The Orphan popped out of the water, looked around him, and saw that he was alive, and realized he was not sinking to the bottom.

The Mom was yelling congratulations, The Dad was looking down, proud that his son listened to his instructions, and The Sisters were jumping up and down in a fit of excitement for their little brother's accomplishment.

That day, The Orphan felt what it was like to have people cheer for him, and if he could get people to cheer for him all the time, maybe they would keep him after all.

From that day forward, every spare moment The Orphan had was spent in the water.

13 A Slap in the Face

"Michael Ray Tabernacky!"

Oh No! The Orphan's head shot up.

It was Bridget, standing in the entryway to The Parents' room.

"That's it. I'm telling Dad! You are in so much trouble!" She had a look of complete rage on her face.

The Orphan gave her a mocking grin.

"What are you smiling at?" She shot him a glance that could melt dry ice.

"You're just angry that you don't look like those girls!" The Orphan lashed out, knowing that sending her into a complete frenzy was the only way he might be able to get out of being tattled on.

If he could just get her to do something that she was not supposed to do, then he could tell her, and the whole thing would end in a stalemate because she wouldn't want to get into trouble either.

Caught up in his own plot, The Orphan didn't see the open hand swinging his way.

Slap!

The Orphan was struck across the face.

His instincts sent him into the nearest corner, knees pulled up to his chest with his reddened face buried in his lap. He balled up as tight as he could and waited for more.

"I'M SORRY. DON'T HIT ME PLEASE!" The Orphan repeated two or three times nervously, rocking back and forth.

His eyes were focused on the shag carpet in total submission. He was sobbing so uncontrollably; he was shaking and couldn't catch his breath.

He was overreacting, but in the couple of years since he had come to this family, no one had ever struck him in the face.

The reality of his violent past came swirling back as he lost track of his surroundings.

"Mike? What happened? It's okay! What is wrong with you?" he heard, as someone touched him on the shoulder.

He tightened, pushing himself even further against the wall, sealing up all cracks that led to another blow to his head or face.

"Mike! It's okay. It's me. Valerie!"

The Orphan stopped rocking back and forth and parted his arms, making a crack to see through to make sure he wasn't being tricked.

He saw Valerie and sprang into her arms, buried his head into her shoulder, and held onto her until he quit sobbing.

"What happened?" Valerie asked with concern.

"Bridget hit me across the face! I told you! I told you family hurts you! No matter how nice they are at first, they always turn mean! She hit me! I was told it would stop. There would be no more! Family lies too! If it's okay to lie and hurt, I can do that! I can lie! I can hurt people!" The Orphan had a frightened and rabid look on his face.

He had made up his mind. He knew how to make people prove that they loved him. He would push them. He would push them like he pushed Bridget, and if they couldn't handle it, they would hurt him like Bridget did; and if they hurt him like Bridget did, then he knew not to trust them ever again.

"Mike!" Valerie raised her voice.

The Orphan snapped out of his anger-induced thoughts.

"Did Bridget catch you looking at this?" Her voice was amused.

The Orphan's expression changed instantly. He was embarrassed and his chubby cheeks were turning rose-red. His shoulders were slumped, mouth gaping.

She was waiting for a response to emerge, but The Orphan could not find one.

"Yes," he finally admitted.

Valerie burst out into an uncontrollable laugh, confusing The Orphan.

"Oh, Mike! She hates these things like Jesus hates Satan. If you ever want to make her mad, just pull one of these puppies out. You will get her going, real quick!" Valerie's voice was amused.

She started half-heartedly flipping through the pages.

"Do you like looking at them, Mike?" She was serious now.

"Yes," The Orphan mumbled, tired of telling people that he liked it and then having them make him feel bad for it.

"So do I, but not for the same reasons. Here, sit with me and we will look at it together." She hopped onto the floor beside him.

"What!" he blurted incredulously.

"Don't look at me like that. I'm not Bridget, and I like to look at them too. These women are beautiful. Who wouldn't want to look at them?" Valerie's facial expressions as she looked at the pictures were of complete admiration.

She pointed at a nude woman in the Playboy she had picked up.

"I am an artist, and artists have been using bodies in the nude since time began. It's a beautiful thing, the body, and I think it should be celebrated."

"Do you know what these are called?" she asked, looking up at him.

The Orphan shook his head no.

"These are boobs or tits, as the boys at my school call them." She was teaching him, he realized. "Aren't they pretty?" Her face was focused on a beautiful woman's bosom.

"Yes," The Orphan agreed, with a smile on his face, the color returning to his cheeks.

"I don't have boobies yet, but when I do, I will be the most beautiful woman in the world. I will be in this magazine and all the cute guys will look at me too. I know you like looking at these pictures, Mike, but you can't let Bridget or Mom and Dad catch you. I won't tell anyone that you look at these, but you have promised that it's our secret. Okay?" Her face was nonjudgmental, and he couldn't sense any deception.

The Orphan nodded his head, spit on his hand, and offered it to Valerie.

"Deal." She spit on her hand and shook his hand.

14 The Promise

Sitting on his bedroom floor eating half a peanut butter and jelly sandwich that he had stuffed in his pillowcase the day before, The Orphan heard a knock on the door. He quickly swallowed the bite and stuffed the rest of his sandwich away for safekeeping.

It was forbidden for him to have food in his room because of all the "little hiding places" The Mom had been finding over the years. The Orphan didn't know why he still stole and hid food. He received three meals a day, plus snacks and desserts to boot, but for some reason, knowing that he had food in his room made him feel safe.

"Who is it?" he responded, satisfied he had gotten rid of all the evidence.

"Can I come in, Michael?"

It was Bridget.

Before he could answer, she opened the door and walked into the room toward him.

Immediately, The Orphan sat up on his bed and backed himself into the corner of his wall.

"I'm not going to hit you, so stop it!" she chided. "I wanted to say I am sorry for hitting you. I will never hit you again. I promise. I was wrong, and I shouldn't have done it! Will you forgive me please?" Her eyes were red and puffy with tears in them.

She looked away when she made eye contact with her little brother, seeing how scared of her he now was.

The Orphan studied her. She was telling the truth, but he wasn't ready to forgive or trust her yet.

He built up the courage to speak and lashed out at her.

"I am always going to look at boobies! You can't stop me. You can hit me, lie, and tell me all you want, but I will always do it!" The Orphan was out of the corner now, leaning toward his sister aggressively. His green eyes were boring right into her, daring her to challenge him, to try and hurt him again.

"Okay," she responded submissively, breaking the gaze he had her locked into.

"Just don't do it around me, and don't let Mom and Dad catch you either." Her voice sounded defeated. She was looking at him again. "Michael?"

She almost always called him Michael. She was the only one in The Family who used his full name without being mad at him.

"You know when I hit you, how much it hurt you? How much did it scare you?" Now her gaze was boring holes into him.

"Yes," he replied uneasily, less certain about himself now.

"When you said what you said, it hurt me like that. Not in the physical way, but you hurt me on the inside. You are right. I don't look like those girls, and I might not ever look like them, but all women are beautiful. All women deserve a man to love and lust after their hearts and bodies. I don't hate these magazines because the women are naked and beautiful."

"Then why do you hate them so much?" The Orphan asked with confusion.

I hate them because they make men think that's what a woman has to look like, and if that is what a woman is supposed to look like, who is going to want women like me?" She had tears running down her cheeks.

The realization of what he had done settled in as he looked into Bridget's red, puffy eyes.

"Will you promise not to say things like that to any woman, not just me? It's really important." Her voice was almost a whisper and her gaze pleading.

The Dad's advice echoed in his mind. "A woman is a precious creation and, in my opinion, the most precious creation the world has to offer. You have to treat them with respect, never lose your temper, make fun of their bodies, or hit them under any circumstances..."

He had disobeyed The Dad, and now he saw the damage it had done to his sister, The Sister that always protected him. Sometimes if she knew he was going to get spanked, she would bend the truth for him and physically place herself between The Dad and him to try to prevent a paddling.

The Orphan was speechless. Bridget had always been the most confident person, besides The Dad, that he had ever met.

But now she was more than depressed; she was demolished. He had attacked her in the only way that could hurt her and now, he wished he would have never done it.

"I promise I won't ever say things like that to any girl or woman again." He shook his head in shame, not even able to look her in the eye.

She sat on the bed, gave The Orphan a kiss on the forehead, and then left the room without another word being said.

It was a promise both of them would keep.

 # Flashbacks

"You owe me $1.25—plus the $5.00."

The Orphan had his head lowered, hand stretched out, and a deep scowl on his face that showed confidence combined with a little irritation.

"I don't think I should have to pay you extra, regardless of whether they were fresh or not!"

Across from the nine-year-old boy was a tall, slender man that smelled of motor oil, beer and bad cologne. He was in his late thirties, with deep, black hair that was starting to gray and thin on both sides of his forehead. His long sleeve shirt was covered in grease, and his hands were black from working on the old pickup that was sitting in the front of his two-door garage. He wore old jeans that had been cut into shorts and big round bifocals that gave him the look of a mad scientist.

"Look, mister, I explained the conditions of our contract before I started the work. You can't just change the terms because you don't think it's fair! Who told you that life is fair anyway? Besides, why would you try to cheat a nine-year-old out of $1.25? Are you really that cheap? Pay up or I will have to get my collector." The Orphan wasn't mad, but he wanted to make sure he handled this right.

"Look, kid... I'm not paying the extra money. Now take your shit and get out of here!" The amused smile had faded on Mr. Roy's face which was starting to turn a shade of red from his irritation.

"Are you sure that this is how you want to handle this situation, mister?" The Orphan wasn't backing down. He knew he was right about this.

"Get the hell out of here, kid!" The man opened his backyard gate and pointed to the blacktop street.

The Orphan got his wagon with all his tools in it and walked through the gate without saying another word to Mr. Roy.

Most kids his age would be afraid, maybe even embarrassed, to talk to an adult in such a way. The Mom and Dad had always told him that kids were meant to be seen, not heard, but this was different.

This was business!

He had provided a much-needed service at a reasonable price, and he was getting cheated by some jerk that thought he was going to break the rules of a perfectly constructed verbal contract. The rules were clearly set in place before the work had begun, and Mr. Roy was not going to get out of it.

The Orphan realized that he was starting to get worked up, so he calmed down using the thought of playing in his room with all his toys. Thinking of playing in his room always made him happy.

The Orphan smiled, in spite of himself.

He had so many toys, he couldn't even play with them these days. It was a stark contrast to his "humble beginnings" of having toys that could only be looked at and not played with.

Toy. The Orphan thought of the word.

That word always made him think of that lady Sarah.

When he had told his parents about Sarah, they had not already known but they had extensive knowledge about her.

They had even shown him a picture that she had given to the social center that was in charge of The Orphan to remember her by.

The picture was exactly how he remembered it.

The two of them were standing around an island table with big grins on their faces.

The picture showed The Orphan standing on top of a step-up stool, looking out over an island bar in the middle of the kitchen. The Orphan had flour all over his face and had the cheesiest grin going from ear to ear. Sarah was looking at him with a mixture of amusement and disbelief.

The Orphan remembered that smile and, for just a brief second, he missed Sarah.

At the time, he had thought that he was going to get into trouble because of the mess that he made. Instead, she just stopped and smiled at how silly he looked with flour plastered all over his face and nose. Sarah even grabbed a handful of the flour and playfully tossed it at him, making him look even more ridiculous than he already did, with a layer of flour caked on top of the mop he called his hair.

The Orphan smiled as he remembered the memory and how hard he had laughed that night. It was the first positive memory that he could remember and, as mean as Sarah was, he loved her for the way she had made him laugh that night.

Knowing that The Parents had this picture also made him wonder how much more they knew about his past that he didn't. If they knew and had pictures of him with Sarah, maybe they knew and had pictures of more things than he remembered.

He often wondered who had taken that picture, but that would have to remain a mystery like so many other things in his life.

When The Orphan finally arrived home, he went straight to The Mom and briefed her on the situation, making sure he recalled even the smallest of details. If he relayed the information right, The Mom would make sure that every minute description of what happened was relayed to The Dad as soon as he got home.

The Orphan also knew that The Dad would help him, no matter what, but if he recruited The Mom, he knew that there would be no delay.

Once he was done recanting the story, The Orphan received the response he had expected.

"Your Dad will take care of it" was all The Mom said and urged, "so go play until he gets home," almost as if she did not have a care in the world.

She went back to what she was doing, which just so happened to be baking something. He could tell that she was trying to hide the scowl on her face from the story he had just told her.

The Orphan knew she was upset and that meant that The Dad's help was on its way.

Satisfied he had done all he could, The Orphan turned around and headed to his room.

As he walked up the stairs, he couldn't help but take in all the aromas of The Mom's cooking.

She was always baking, sewing, or cleaning, and today she just so happened to be baking chocolate chip cookies. He grabbed a couple on his way out of the kitchen before she could notice and turned the corner out of the kitchen to head up the stairs.

He no longer needed to hide food out of hunger, but he had been doing it so long that it just came second nature to him. As a matter of fact, he was eating so much and getting so big that some of the kids at school were starting to call him fat.

The Orphan furrowed his eyebrows in irritation.

That's only because they don't know what it's like to truly be hungry, The Orphan thought to himself.

He was not only unashamed of his weight gain; he was grateful for it.

So many times, he had fallen asleep hungry and thirsty. So many times, he had wondered if he was going to get another meal or if someone was going to give him something to drink. He was never going to let that happen to him again.

"Thank You, God," The Orphan mumbled under his breath as he climbed the stairs and walked down the hallway to his room.

16 Blood Brother

When he got to his room, clothes were strewn everywhere. Toys littered the floor, and it immediately brought a smirk to his face.

The Parents hated the fact that his room was always messy, but there were more important things to do than clean his room and do chores.

If Sarah ever saw this, he would have gotten the beating of his life! The smile faded as the memory of how long it took him to heal from that beating came to mind.

The positive memories of Sarah vanished upon recalling how hard she could hit for such a small adult.

"She may have given me my first smile, but that was all she was good for," he reminded himself.

The Orphan quickly went through all the memories of his other homes, parents, and social workers. He always made it a point to remind himself of what had happened to him, who had done it, and how it made him feel.

Tears always rolled down his cheeks when he thought of those memories, but for a reason he did not know, it always helped him come to grips with the fact that his real parents did not want him.

Things were different here, though. The Parents provided and cared for him like he was their child, but that only helped temporarily. There were no memories of a first step, first word, or even the simple recollection of what he was like as a baby. These were things that The Parents could never provide him, so no matter how hard he tried, there would always be a void that could never be filled.

In the meantime, he had to continue to test them as a "REAL" child would.

He knew for a fact that, no matter what, The Parents would never send The Sisters to a community center. Understanding this, The Orphan took every opportunity he could to see if they would do the same for him.

He had more than tested the boundaries of this new family; he had shattered them. It didn't take long for him to learn what he would get in trouble for, how far he could push the lines, and once that line was crossed, he knew exactly what he needed to do to get out of trouble again.

Once The Orphan was inside his room, he closed the door, sat on the floor, and reached under a pair of dirty jeans to pull out a Snowball from one of his many hiding places and replaced it with the chocolate chip cookies he had swiped moments earlier from the kitchen.

It always amazed him how such a thing could be made. It was like a marshmallow with coconut flakes glued to it, but you could peel it like an orange to reveal a chocolate core. Then, once you bit into the chocolate core, there was frosting inside, and when you bit into all three layers at once... it was total bliss!

The first half of the Snowball was gone before the thought was finished and, just before he could take a bite of the second half, his door opened.

"Busted, little brother. You know the rules. Cough it up!" Valerie had her hand out like a beggar, but her face reflected anything but meekness.

"Dad said sugar hurts you, and I'm not supposed to give you any." The Orphan knew this argument wouldn't work.

It never did.

Valerie just stood there with an outstretched hand, looking at him expectantly.

The Orphan handed over the second half of the pink Snowball with a solemn look on his face.

"Will you take a shot of insulin before you eat it, just to make sure your blood sugar goes back down?" he asked, more than a little ashamed of himself.

This was not new territory. For six years, The Dad had been teaching him about Valerie's diabetes and, for six years, The Orphan had been trying to protect Valerie from the one thing that could kill her.

"Sugar."

The Orphan held out his pinky, waiting for her to finish sealing the deal.

Valerie reached out, grabbed his pinky with a smile, and without hesitation gave him a kiss on the cheek as she walked out of his room.

The Orphan remembered all the different ways Valerie had come up with to secure a deal in their short past together. He even recalled the time that they had cut their hands with a knife to become "blood brother and sister."

The Orphan remembered the look on Valerie's face the day they had shook hands with blood dripping from their hands.

"It takes thirty seconds of our blood mixing to make it official," The Orphan remembered her saying.

She was so excited once the ceremony was complete, but they would never be able to do something like that again.

With a new disease that The Mom and The Dad called AIDS, they had told both him and The Sisters that they were not to use spit or blood brother handshakes with anyone, including each other.

That didn't stop them from coming up with other ways to validate the back door deals they made so often.

The Orphan continued to ponder Valerie's situation as he sat there.

Valerie loved candy as much as The Orphan did, but it made her get sick. The Dad had taught him how to take care of her in case of an emergency, but over time they started to use that knowledge so Valerie could eat what she wanted.

It wasn't that hard. If her blood sugar dropped to a certain point, all she had to do was eat something healthy; and if it went too high, all she had to do was take the correct dosage of insulin.

The Dad had told The Orphan that insulin was produced from the pancreas, and for whatever reason, Valerie's pancreas just stopped working. No one knew why or how and, truth be told, it wouldn't have mattered if they had known.

Valerie would never be normal, and in the end, that was all that mattered to her.

The Orphan could remember The Dad describing the day they had to rush Valerie to the hospital because she had blacked out on a hot summer day.

"It was the scariest day of my life, son. She just dropped to the floor, right in front of us. Not only did we not know what to do but, for the first time, I felt helpless and had to rely on doctors to give me advice; and that, son, is never a good thing." There was always a sense of regret in The Dad's voice when he talked about Valerie's diabetes.

The Dad was always weary of physicians. From all the scars on his body and medication that he had to take all the time for his pain, The Orphan could see why.

Valerie's disease only increased that skepticism.

Bloomington was a small town, and its resources in the medical field were limited. When the doctors did finally find out what was wrong with Valerie, they did not know how to treat or guide her through her disease. Not only was little known about diabetes, but whatever was known about treatment for the condition only seemed to make her worse.

The Orphan had always known that the disease was affecting his sister physically, but for the first time, he could see how it was affecting her psychologically.

The world had her trapped, and everywhere she turned, and the more she tried to fit in, the worse it seemed to get for her. She could not escape her disease's reality and was defenseless to stop its progress.

He recalled what she had told him one day, not so long ago.

"This is my world, Mikey, and you need to remember that when you feel sorry for yourself. Your nightmares exist only when you close your eyes; mine exist while mine are open."

She said it with such sadness, The Orphan wished he could take the disease from her, so she could go back to being normal with her family. It didn't matter what happened to him because all he wanted was for his sister to play with other kids, smile the way she used to, and be the positive influence on him that she had always been; but all that seemed a distant memory right now.

It was almost as if, day by day, she was starting to lose hope altogether.

Just when The Orphan didn't think things could get worse for Valerie, the unthinkable happened.

People at school were starting to be mean to her.

 **Fight Club**

Teachers were upset that Valerie had mandatory "special snack breaks" when the other kids didn't. The parents of the other kids didn't understand the disease she carried and thought she was contagious, so they wouldn't let their kids play with her anymore. She was alienated, humiliated, and picked on.

Her diabetes also made her an easy target for the AIDS epidemic hysteria that was all over the news, and kids started spreading rumors that they would die if any of her blood got on them.

School fights turned into a daily occurrence. The Dad had to start teaching Valerie how to protect herself from the kids that would gang up on her and throw rocks at her after school.

It didn't take long for Valerie to become feared for her fighting skills and soon, her bullies refocused their energy on easier prey.

But the damage had already been done.

Valerie was an outsider, cast into exile by her peers. In a way, it was worse than The Orphan's situation. At least he could actually say he had always been an outsider, but Valerie used to be one of them; she played, joked, had sleepovers, and built hopes and dreams based off their friendships together. When her disease became public, they threw her out like a rotten dish in the refrigerator.

She tried to pretend that it did not bother her, but The Orphan knew her better.

The Caretaker and the Protector

His sister was completely demolished, and she had shared with The Orphan on more than one occasion that she didn't want to live anymore. He did his best to make her feel better about herself, but she needed friends besides him. She needed another person her age to hug her, tell her she was a normal teenage girl, and be there for her at her lowest.

That person just didn't seem to exist for Valerie.

The Orphan watched this happen slowly as the years rolled by, and he admired his sister for the fighter she had become and the determination she had to never let her disease control her life.

The Dad had said that it was The Orphan's job to protect Valerie. To keep her from breaking her diet and to always be the voice of reason for her, but Valerie was his best friend. So, when she wanted something, he gave it to her, no matter what it was and no matter how guilty he felt.

To try to balance the role he had in destroying her carefully planned diet, he never showed her where his stash was and he always snuck into her room to remove the candy and junk food SHE would stash. He understood why she hid food. The reason was different than his own, but it was a good reason, nonetheless, so The Orphan tried not to take everything—just the most harmful foods.

He would also monitor her insulin bottles to make sure she was taking her three shots a day, with the correct dosage. It had gotten to be so much work that, on more than one occasion, he just wanted to spill the beans to The Dad so he could march up there, clean out her room, and straighten her out, but he never did.

The Orphan thought back to the first day he was adopted, and The Dad had told and shown him about Valerie's disease. He remembered what The Dad had said.

"She is a strong little girl, Michael. Learn from her because both of you are unique in your own special way."

In the end, it was that sentence that kept him from telling. The Orphan knew all too well what it was like to be so different that no one liked you, and when you put someone in that situation, they "have" to have something that can make them feel good about themselves. For The Orphan, that was food and The Dad's magazines.

For Valerie, it was sugar and junk food.

It had been a long time since the day that The Dad methodically showed him how to measure, inject insulin, and destroy Valerie's hypodermic needles. Only a couple of years after they had adopted him, The Dad had him inject Valerie with one of her needles. He could tell that the shots hurt her more than poking her finger to take her blood levels because she would always have tears in her eyes after she was injected with the insulin.

Valerie was in charge of her own injections, but The Dad would always have The Orphan do it every now and then to make sure that his son remembered how to do it and was doing it correctly. The only difference between now and then was Valerie would inject herself in the thigh now, instead of the buttocks.

Valerie had told him that The Dad had her start injecting that way so she wouldn't have to expose her backside to The Orphan anymore. He had an inkling that it had to do with him passing out that first night they brought him home, but no one talked to him about it.

He wanted to ask The Dad if that was the reason, but he had gotten into so much trouble the past couple years in school that he tried not to confront The Dad on anything.

As he waited for The Dad to get home, he started to think of some of the bigger things he had done to get into trouble the past few years.

School Times

The Orphan's first couple of years in school were rough ones.

Most of the kids thought he was weird for being adopted. The rest would make comments about his sister's disease to try to pick a fight with him. To make things worse, he didn't seem to be as smart as the other kids in his class. He couldn't read or pronounce words that the other kids seemed to know with ease, and he didn't know how to draw pictures or how to say the alphabet in the correct order.

When The Parents had taken him to his first day of kindergarten at Bluffview Elementary School... it was not only hard; it was a culture shock.

Sitting in one place for hours at a time was out of the question, which meant his teachers always labeled him a "troublemaker," tried to put him into "special programs," and at one point even tried to have a doctor give him drugs to calm him down.

This made him feel even more out of place and, of course, with kids being kids, they labeled him "the dumb one" in the class.

Making things more difficult was the fact that the kids around him had also grown up and played together since birth. The Orphan soon found out that there was little room for a migrating gypsy like himself. There were a few kids he could hang out and play with, but none of them he really trusted.

All the kids that he played soccer and other sports with were semi-nice to him while he was at practice or a game, but other than that, most kept a good distance.

That left The Dad for The Orphan to talk to.

The Dad was his best friend, if you could call it that. He taught The Orphan when to stand tall, to pick his battles, and when to admit when he was wrong. Every day, The Dad would carefully coach The Orphan on how to deal with bullying, his anger issues, and anything else that was bothering him at the time. He refused to give The Orphan any drugs that were meant to help him or put him in any secondary classes designed for "special kids."

The Orphan liked his talks with The Dad, but it didn't really seem to help with his grades or attitude that much.

At times, when The Dad was frustrated, he would often tell The Orphan that his "full time job in life consisted of almost nothing but getting his son to move onto the next grade," and, "whatever I tell you goes in one ear, and out the other." The Dad was never angry when he said those things, but he was disappointed, which to The Orphan was worse than anger.

Guilt started to make The Orphan change the way he communicated with The Parents. He started becoming more distant and reclusive, and to make matters worse, he no longer had anyone to confide in. The Dad would always be The Dad, but it almost seemed that he was becoming more trouble than he was worth to this family.

Depression was starting to set in.

He wanted to be a good son for The Dad, get good grades, and be the best in sports, but his actions always seemed to do the complete opposite of what he knew would make The Dad proud. The harder he tried, the worse it seemed to get for him.

The Orphan's mind wandered to a couple of the things he had done the past couple years to push The Dad's buttons. It was easy to find an instance that could quickly rekindle The Dad's irritation if he were reminded.

 Santa Clause

Santa walked into the room one day in the middle of class, and The Orphan immediately became suspicious. Kids were screaming and giggling all around him, but there was something about this Santa that was off.

For one, there was the limp.

"When did Santa ever limp on TV?"

Then there were the thick glasses.

Again, Santa never wore glasses unless he was by the fire reading and eating his milk and cookies.

And then, there was the eye contact Santa made with him as soon as he walked into the room.

Why would Santa search me out and hold my gaze if he did not recognize who he was looking at?

The Orphan was almost sure he had the riddle solved, but he had to make certain before he took any action and shared his discovery.

With a smile on his face, The Orphan placed himself toward the back of the line, wanting some time to watch this so-called... "Santa."

Doubt flooded over The Orphan as he got closer. Santa had not made eye contact since he had walked into the room, and now that he was sitting down, there was nothing to remind The Orphan about the limp he had noticed earlier when Santa first walked in the room.

What The Orphan did see was all his classmates tearing through presents and walking away from Santa with a big smile on their faces from the gifts that they had been given.

Gifts that he selfishly wanted to keep for himself.

Then the moment arrived. It was his turn.

He walked up to Santa and was greeted with a "Ho! Ho! Ho!" and "Merry Christmas!" from the overly enthusiastic man dressed in the Santa suit.

The Orphan hopped onto Santa's lap and immediately started studying his face. "What's your name, little boy?" Santa asked with a jolly grin, looking at The Orphan with a nervous twitch in his eye.

"Dad?" The Orphan mouthed, low enough that no one else could hear.

"I'm Santa Claus, not Dad; but what's your name, son?" Santa nervously chuckled and broke eye contact as soon as he heard The Orphan mouth the word, "Dad."

Upon hearing the word, "son," The Orphan was positive who Santa really was, and without warning, he grabbed Santa's beard and pulled it down, revealing the clean-shaven face of The Dad.

All hell broke loose in the class.

"Santa isn't real!" a kid screamed from behind The Orphan.

In an instant, the classroom was in chaos, with angry, screaming boys and crying girls sobbing on the floor in melodramatic fashion. The Orphan looked at The Dad in humiliation and shame, but when he made eye contact, The Orphan was surprised to see that The Dad wasn't mad or irritated, but rather sympathetic and understanding.

It was an innocent mistake, but one that both of them knew would further alienate him from the rest of the class. Kids remember these kinds of things, and kids aren't nearly as forgiving as adults are.

The Orphan would go the rest of the school year without a single friend in his class, and there was nothing he was going to be able to do about it.

Later that day when The Dad asked what had tipped him off that it was him impersonating Santa, The Orphan's response was immediate.

"Remember when you adopted me and you said, 'I am your Dad, this is your Mom, and those are your Sisters'? You also told me that I would always be your son. Well, you had the same tone of voice when you said the words, 'dad' and 'son.'

"I was so excited it was you. I didn't even think that the other kids wouldn't be happy too. I would much rather see you than Santa anyway, but I guess most kids can't say that. I didn't mean to ruin everything; I just wanted to show everyone that my dad was Santa."

The Orphan was crying as he remembered the looks of the other children in the classroom. He had destroyed the image of Santa that day for some in that classroom, and the other parents were scrambling to figure out how they were going to explain to their children that "Old Saint Nick" was, in fact, Mr. Tabernacky from The Camino Placers.

 # Knives Out

The Orphan had always been fascinated with knives, even though he always seemed to cut himself by accident with them. The Dad had even prohibited him from having any knives because of the one-inch laceration he gave himself while carving wood sometime back.

After The Mom had cleaned the cut with rubbing alcohol and closed it with superglue and a butterfly stitch Band-Aid, The Dad had promptly marched up to The Orphan's room and confiscated all of his knives, but the punishment was of little consequence.

With The Orphan, you could never truly confiscate ALL of his collection of anything.

He had learned long ago that you never put all your valuables in the same place. It was best to have two or maybe three different stashes at any given time. This rule applied for anything The Orphan thought was important.

Throughout his whole life, people had been taking things from him. Whether it was his body, belongings, or happiness, it always seemed that people wanted what he had. The Orphan did not know if life was this way for everyone, but one thing he knew for sure, at a very young age, was that he was going to be the only one that looked after him.

It didn't take long for The Orphan to find The Dad's hiding place for his knives, and he was quite proud of the new hiding place he had chosen.

The genius of *this* hiding place was it was exactly where The Dad had hidden them, which in this case just happened to be under The Dad's *Playboy*s.

Located in The Dad's spare drawer underneath the waterbed, The Orphan was actually excited that he had found them there.

It meant that not only did The Dad NOT know about his son looking at his *Playboys,* but it also meant that Bridget had kept her word and didn't tell The Dad that The Orphan had looked at his magazines.

The Orphan was content to just leave the knives there until The Dad gave them back. He didn't know when that might happen, but it didn't matter much.

One day, a kid had gotten expelled from school for getting caught bringing a knife to school; it automatically sparked The Orphan's competitive side. He instantly became convinced he could have gotten away with it.

That day at recess, he had told Dustin that same thing.

"If that would have been me, man, I would have gotten away with it." The Orphan was in full presentation mode.

Dustin was the only person who would hang out with The Orphan that year, but they were not in the same class together, so they only got to talk and play at morning recess.

"Mike, you are so full of it, bro. All you do is brag about how good you are at things—how good you are at that and this. I am sick of hearing it! I want to see you do it."

Dustin was from Florida. Kids would joke and say he was number three, meaning that he was one of the three black kids in all of Bloomington.

It wasn't a prejudiced thing, but The Orphan could tell it bothered Dustin. It was just a common joke in the community that there were no black people... anywhere! Kids being kids used this to leverage the social structure of the school, dictating who was on the in, and who was on the out. At this moment, Dustin was on the out, and that was why he had to hang out with The Orphan. Dustin knew this and so did The Orphan, but over time they started to develop a real friendship.

Dustin's skin was very dark, and he had even blacker, curly hair. He was skinny and always slouched when he walked. Besides the black vs. white jokes that were so commonplace, some of the kids would make fun of his height and the way he talked. The Orphan would catch Dustin actually trying to shrink to a shorter height and talk a different way when the other kids came around in order to try to change the image so many had of him.

The greatest thing about Dustin, though, was his sense of humor. The Orphan had never encountered someone who could make him and everyone else laugh so much. In many ways, Dustin taught The Orphan how to laugh at life, even when there was nothing to laugh at.

Dustin was always cracking jokes. He had black jokes, white jokes, dirty, clean and in-between jokes, one-liners and twelve-liners. He would light up when he told them, too. It reminded The Orphan of Eddie Murphy in his stand-up shows on late-night HBO.

The Orphan could even picture Dustin in front of a crowd with those bright white teeth, black agate pupils, and a smile that could electrify a room. He would imagine Dustin bringing the house down and people would chant, "Encore!" – and beg for more, but for the moment, all The Orphan wanted to do was prove that he could do what he said he would do.

"I'll bring it tomorrow!" The Orphan blurted out before he could stop himself.

"You will not." Dustin was convinced this was another one of The Orphan's attention grabbers.

"I will. You'll see." The Orphan took a bite of his snack that The Mom had packed for his recess.

"Here." Dustin handed The Orphan something.

"What is it?" The Orphan asked, eyebrows furrowed and eyes focusing on the small object handed to him.

"It's a raisin," Dustin said with a warm smile.

"Thanks," The Orphan shot back.

Something tweaked The Orphan's memory and, just before he popped the raisin in his mouth, he stopped himself and took a second look at the dried up "fruit." Then he remembered the smile on Dustin's face.

I know that smile!

The Orphan punched Dustin on the arm as hard as he could.

"You are disgusting! What the hell kind of friend are you anyway? This isn't a raisin; this is the scab you just picked off your grimy knee, you ASS!" The Orphan took the balled-up scab and threw it at Dustin's open mouth, hoping it would land inside.

It would have if Dustin wouldn't have turned his head to the side just before it flew in.

Dustin was laughing so hard; he fell on his back from where they were both seated on the ground.

"I almost had you, man. I would have told everyone. That would have been the most disgusting thing I have ever seen in my life!" Dustin couldn't stop laughing, even as the recess bell rung and they stood up to go to their classes.

The Orphan grabbed his snack box and jacket that The Dad had gotten him last Christmas and trotted to Ms. May's class.

The next day, The Orphan was a nervous wreck. He had taken the knife from the drawer, brought it to school, and had been putting Dustin off all day. The burden of possibly being expelled was eating at him.

If he got caught, The Dad would kill him, and The Orphan was convinced it would be a slow death.

Like the ones The Dad always talked about in his war stories. He winced as the thought came to mind.

On the other hand, there was Dustin.

If The Orphan didn't pony up the knife and prove that he could get away with it, then Dustin would run his mouth off to everyone in school that The Orphan was a "chicken."

Being called a "chicken" didn't bother The Orphan, until he saw another guy named Michael in a movie called *Back to the Future* that taught him: under no circumstances should you let someone call you a chicken!

When he asked The Dad about it, all he would say is, "Words never hurt anyone."

The Orphan couldn't disagree more. Words did hurt.

There was a loud ring, announcing the final recess of the day.

The Orphan walked over to his usual meeting place by the basketball hoops, where he knew Dustin would already be waiting for him. The Orphan turned the corner, and as he got closer to Dustin, he could see that he had a big grin on his face.

The Orphan knew that Dustin was positive that he was going to win the bet and that The Orphan had chickened out.

"Okay. I am ready to show it to you." The Orphan was sweating, despite the chilly temperature, and his voice was a little shaky from his nerves being rattled.

"You don't have it." Dustin didn't even bother putting the sentence into question form.

Without a word, The Orphan reached into his pocket, pulled out his knife, unlatched the blade, and locked it into place.

"Yes, I do. See," The Orphan almost whispered, glancing around to make sure no one was looking.

The Orphan was knocked flat on his back without warning.

"KNIFE!!" someone shouted.

Dustin was on top of him, pounding his wrist against the pavement.

"HE'S GOT A KNIFE! HELP!" Dustin shouted at the top of his lungs.

"What are you doing!" The Orphan seethed through clenched teeth at the betrayal.

"Stop struggling, man. I am going to hurt you if you don't. I am bigger and you can't get away." Dustin was right, of course, but The Orphan wasn't putting up much of a fight because of the confusion.

The Orphan was crushed. Dustin had betrayed him, and he had no idea why.

The teachers came and quickly pinned The Orphan to the ground, restraining his arms and legs, pinning them to the ground and preventing almost any movement.

Something inside The Orphan snapped.

He started screaming and kicking uncontrollably.

The teachers could no longer contain him. Soon, they were all dog piled on top of The Orphan, trying desperately to hold him down.

It didn't matter.

The Orphan was in a crazed fit. He started to roll like an alligator, tearing his clothes and lacerating his skin as he rolled over and over in his mindless fit of rage. He bit and clawed at anything he could, ignoring any instructions or threats being directed his way from the people screaming at him.

If The Orphan could have seen it, he would have noticed the complete shock and horror from the students and teachers alike. Dustin, no longer proud of his self-proclaimed heroism, had fled the scene in complete horror of what he was responsible for.

Soon, all the voices started to fade as memories of being pinned down at a different time in a different place came racing back.

The Orphan was suddenly freezing. When he opened his eyes again, he was strapped to a cold, metal bed.

 The Blackout

He was somewhere else, but he didn't know where. Dustin was gone, as well as all the teachers trying to pin him to the ground. There were no kids, no playgrounds; just him in a room, strapped to a metal bed.

Suddenly, there was pain. Excruciating pain!

The Orphan tried arching his back but couldn't. He could feel screams travel up his throat, but something was stuffed in his mouth, preventing the sound from coming out.

Then something was cutting into his back.

He could feel his flesh split apart, and all he could do was close his eyes and whimper.

A stream of warm but cool liquid flowed down his back and curved around to his little belly. He didn't know how long he had been bleeding, but the puddle of blood would tickle his belly in between sobs.

That small tickle was all it took to help The Orphan to escape into a better world, one away from his body and the things adults did to it.

While physically he was being cut to pieces, mentally, he was playing with toys, eating all kinds of food, and hugging The Dad who was protecting him, embracing The Mom who would care for his wounds, and hiding behind his sisters who would hunt down, "whoever or whatever did this to him."

He was in front of his neighbors, asking them if he could mow their lawn or pull their weeds, and recalled drinking the cold lemonade and ice water on a hot summer workday.

Then there was "The Rock."

The Orphan would climb out of his window almost every sunset and sit on the roof of his house, watching the sun disappear behind Shiprock. It was his favorite memory. It was the memory that brought him home.

"HOME." The word came to The Orphan's lips as the memory faded.

Suddenly, The Orphan could feel another presence.

Something was trying to communicate with him, but he didn't know who they were or what they were trying to communicate.

A single word came to The Orphan.

"CHOICE."

Then he blacked out.

23 Unintended Consequences

The Orphan bit into a Twizzlers as he finished the thought, sitting alone on his bedroom floor.

He hadn't told anyone about the flashback because of the promise he had made to The Social Worker.

"The Mom and Dad wouldn't want him if they found out." That is what he had been told.

So, he kept it himself; he protected Dustin by telling all The Adults that he brought the knife because someone had called him a chicken and he learned on TV that you couldn't let anyone in life do that to you.

As usual, The Dad came to his son's rescue. He was spared the expulsion but would be labeled as a "violent child."

In the end, The Orphan did get suspended.

The Dad made him spend his three days of school suspension picking up dog poop for all his clients for free as punishment.

A total loss of $150.00 in wages for that week and, on top of that, The Orphan had to agree to go to a school-sponsored "counseling group for kids."

The Dad took away his television and all non-family-time TV watching until he could learn the difference between "reality and fantasy," as The Mom put it.

The flashback of the metal bed and cutting kept creeping back into his head, no matter how hard he tried to get them out.

Something else happened to The Orphan during Dustin's betrayal, however. The Law of Unintended Consequences was in full motion as the physical signs of trauma started to show, along with the mental.

It was that flashback, while being held down to the ground by the teachers, that triggered The Orphan's nightmares. It was these nightmares that gave The Orphan his new bladder problems.

After that day, The Dad had to get up every night, wake The Orphan up, and make him go to the bathroom before tucking him back into bed.

The Orphan would lie and tell him he didn't know why he was so emotional and why he was having problems with sleeping and bedwetting.

The doctors blamed it on malnutrition during his infancy and assured The Mom and Dad it would go away with time.

The Orphan would always let them believe this, so they didn't ask any questions.

Truth of the matter was, he was having nightmares so terrible, he would wake up with a wet bed—not just from urine, but cold sweat as well. From head to toe, there was not a pore dry, as he would wake up, shaking and freezing.

Soon, The Dad had to wake up three times a night so The Orphan wouldn't wet his bed. Like a true soldier, he would set his alarm and make the climb up the tri-level house. To make matters more difficult, The Dad had to take each step one-by-one, due to the artificial knees in both his legs, preventing easy movement.

The guilt The Orphan felt for The Dad having to do this nagged at him every night, making things worse.

After all, who wants a bedwetter for a son?

After several months, The Mom noticed the wet spots on the pillowcase where her little son laid his head every night.

She realized immediately her son was dealing with more than a bladder issue. Her son was trying to heal from something terrible. Something he wasn't telling anyone. She sensed it, and she knew something different needed to happen in order to help The Orphan get over whatever he was dealing with.

Instinctively, she already knew what needed to be done.

One night, The Mom and Dad let him fall asleep in their room.

There had been a big earthquake in a place called "California." The Mom asked The Orphan to sit and watch the news coverage with her.

"It's a tragic day, Michael. It will be a day marked in history forever. Let's pray for those in need." Her voice was so calm, yet there seemed to be pain in it.

Without another word, The Orphan climbed atop the waterbed and laid his head down onto her lap. This was always how he sat with her in church, so it seemed fitting for this moment as well.

The Mom started to gently run her fingers through The Orphan's hair, messaging his scalp in the process.

The Orphan loved it when The Mom did this to him.

In seconds, he was sound asleep.

When The Dad got home, The Mom talked him into letting The Orphan sleep with them to see if it would help.

That night, for the first time in a long time, The Orphan didn't have a single nightmare or bed-wetting accident.

Night after night the nine-year-old would make his way down the stairs to his parents' room, climb onto the waterbed, and lay in between The Parents. He felt protected with The Dad next to him— and loved having The Mom right on the other side.

Such a simple gesture and an even simpler memory but, for the first time, The Orphan finally got to feel what it felt like to sleep next to a real mom and dad.

Soon after that, "three times a night potty breaks" turned into two, two turned into one, and then—they were gone altogether.

The night he could sleep in his bed again, he was so proud of himself.

He was no longer a "bed-wetter," and he could sleep in his own bed like a normal boy his age.

The Orphan finished his Twizzler with tears running down his cheeks, as he sat there on his floor.

"Ya. Definitely a tough few years," he blurted out loud to himself.

He heard The Dad walk in the front door, followed by some unintelligible conversation between The Parents.

It wasn't long before The Orphan heard the all-too-familiar thumping of The Dad climbing up the stairs to his room, before the room to his door was opened, and The Dad came walking in.

"Okay, son. Tell me what happened," was all he said as he closed the bedroom door behind him.

Once The Orphan recounted his story and answered The Dad's questions, the decision to visit Mr. Roy was made immediately.

24 The Collections Department

Knock, Knock, Knock!! The Dad's hand respectfully banged against the hard wood door.

The door opened a few seconds later, and Mr. Roy was looking directly at The Dad.

"Mr. Roy?" The Dad sounded off.

"Yes." Mr. Roy answered.

"Do you recognize this boy, Mr. Roy?" The voice was calm but firm.

Mr. Roy didn't hesitate.

"I thought I told you to never come back, kid!" Mr. Roy's facial expression turned angry in an instant, as he looked down and saw The Orphan standing there looking up at him.

"Oh, believe me, Mr. Roy, he won't be. I just wanted to make sure that this all got worked out in the proper fashion." Again, The Dad's voice was calm.

"It's worked out all right. This kid tried to gouge me for extra money when I already paid him. I told him to take a hike, and I'll tell you the same thing if you don't get off my property!"

Mr. Roy was irate and was starting to get aggressive.

"Mr. Roy. Did my son explain to you that it was an extra twenty-five cents for every fresh one—in addition to the five dollars for the rest of your yard?" The Dad was all business.

He was squared off in front of Mr. Roy in a non-threatening way, ignoring the threats and irritation coming from the half-drunk man standing in front of him.

"Oh, I see, you must be here to collect the bill for this little shit!" Mr. Roy's voice was mocking and condescending toward The Dad as he pointed at The Orphan without looking at him.

In the next moment, Mr. Roy was in his front yard, flat on his back.

The Dad walked over to Mr. Roy, picked him up by the collar of his shirt, and lifted him back to his feet like a limp ragdoll so he could look the man squarely in the face.

"Mr. Roy. I don't like profanity directed toward my son. Did or did my son not explain the terms of the agreement?" The Dad's tone was sharp, with no hint of anger in it.

The Orphan hadn't even seen what The Dad had done to throw Mr. Roy out of the doorway into the yard. It happened so fast; The Orphan could not recall the moves.

"Of course he did, but I'm not going to pay for it! Take your hands off me!" Mr. Roy tried to shake The Dad's grip, but to no avail.

There was a loud "Thump!"

This time, Mr. Roy was in the middle of the neighborhood street!

He had a scraped-up arm and his button-down shirt was ripped on the forearm.

The Dad was advancing his way over to where he was sprawled.

Seeing that The Dad was heading his way, Mr. Roy tried to scramble back to his feet to defend himself but failed before The Dad reached him.

The Dad stood just out of striking distance from where Mr. Roy was propped up on one elbow on the asphalt; the other arm was elevated in a blocking form, as if ready to protect his face from a downward blow.

The Orphan's heart was racing with adrenaline. He had no idea how The Dad could send Mr. Roy flying like that into the street, but it had happened, nonetheless.

He was starting to feel like he was in one of the action movies he saw on TV all the time.

"It's just a FUCKING dollar!" Mr. Roy yelled.

Upon hearing the profanity, The Dad balled up his fist and started to advance.

"Okay! Okay! Here is the money!" Mr. Roy was fumbling for his wallet while trying to crawl away at the same time.

He pulled out a dollar and handed it to The Dad, then reached into his side pocket to pull out the remaining balance of twenty-five cents.

He handed it to The Dad, his hands shaking.

"Mr. Roy, are you forgetting something?" The Dad asked, calm as ever.

"I paid him the money he was owed!" Mr. Roy snapped.

"Mr. Roy, he performed that work for you, and you failed to pay him promptly. I am here to collect the additional interest accrued as well as the original balance. Call it my fee."

"Are you shitting me?" Mr. Roy was flabbergasted.

The Dad's fist came back up.

"Wait! Okay. I'll pay. All I have is a five in my wallet, though." Mr. Roy was frantically reaching into his back pocket for his wallet again. He pulled out a crumpled up five and held it out at arm's length to The Dad.

"Sounds about right!" The Dad responded.

As fast as the money was there, it was gone, snatched up by The Dad's lightning-quick hands.

So fast, in fact, that even Mr. Roy was surprised that the five-dollar bill had disappeared so quickly.

"Can I go now?" Mr. Roy asked, as respectfully as his pride would let him.

"I think you need to do one more thing, Mr. Roy." The Dad demanded in a flat tone as he finally stood up again.

"What?" Mr. Roy sounded resigned.

"Mr. Roy, it's not a very good example for a boy this age to see a full-grown man break an agreement and then treat him, and another man, with such disrespect. Wouldn't you agree?" The Dad's gaze was boring holes into Mr. Roy.

Mr. Roy rolled his eyes and gave a long deep sigh.

"Look, kid..."

"Mike." The Dad kept his cool and clarified. "His name, Mr. Roy, is Mike."

"Look, Mike," Mr. Roy corrected himself. "I apologize to you, and I hope that you will not take this as an example of how adults should treat kids." He looked uncomfortable, like he had just been chided by his mother.

The Orphan didn't skip a beat.

"It's okay, Mr. Roy. I hope that you were happy with the work that was completed, even though we had a little disagreement. My dad says disagreements are a part of business, so that just makes this business, not personal. Right?" The Orphan had confidence in his voice because The Dad had taught him how to do this, and he was excited to use it in real life for the first time.

The Orphan had a look of triumph on his face and a smile from ear to ear; showing the big deep dimples in his cheeks that so many adults seemed to love to pinch.

Mr. Roy couldn't help but smile back.

"Yes, Mike, you are right, and I thank you for reminding me of that." Mr. Roy was no longer angry.

Apparently, The Dad's bill-collecting efforts had sobered him up a little. His tone was appreciative and respectful now.

"Mr. Tabernacky, I apologize to you as well. That's a special boy you have, and I think I am safe in saying, he's got a mind for business. He did a good job, and I will pay extra for the fresh crap to be picked up on my lawn any day!" Mr. Roy was smiling at The Orphan as he spoke the words.

Before The Dad could say anything, The Orphan had a business card out of his pocket and in Mr. Roy's hand.

"You can call on Mike's Pooper Scooper Business anytime, Mr. Roy. If you'll pay up, I pick up— all the poop in your yard!"

With that, all three of them stood in the middle of the street laughing. Mr. Roy and The Dad shook hands, and they all parted ways.

As soon as they were out of earshot:

"How did you throw him around like that?" The Orphan was enthusiastic. "He was your size, but it was like he weighed nothing, and you were so awesome! Can you teach me to do that? What was that move called? It was just like in the movies where the good guy knocks out the bad guy. You have to teach me to do that! Dad. Please. I want to fight like you!" The Orphan was so excited, he was almost jumping up and down.

"Calm down, son." The Dad was laughing, proudly looking at his son.

The Dad slowed down his pace, started easing closer to The Orphan, and before The Orphan could react...

"I did it like this!"

The Orphan was lifted off the ground and turned upside down.

"Sometimes you have to shake the money they owe you out of 'em!" The Dad was holding him by his legs, shaking him, just like they did in all the cartoons he saw on Saturday mornings.

The Orphan was laughing so hard, he almost peed his pants! Everything that he had in his pockets was falling out onto the street, and The Dad's other hand was digging into his ribs, tickling his exposed torso.

"DAD! DAD! Okay, I give up! Put me down, Dad!" The Orphan was begging in a fit of giggles.

The Dad flipped him back around and set him on his feet.

As The Orphan was putting all his belongings back into his pocket, The Dad walked over to the side of the street and eased himself onto the curb.

The Orphan always marveled that The Dad could overcome his handicap and function just like everyone else around him. Others just felt sorry for The Dad, but The Orphan was proud of everything about The Dad, including his handicaps.

"Come over and sit next to me, son." The Dad was looking at him. He still had a smile on his face, his white teeth showing through a grin that put a smile on his son's face.

Once The Orphan had finished putting everything into his pockets, he made his way over to where The Dad was seated and waited for whatever The Dad had to say.

"Son, Mr. Roy did something that was very bad. I hate liars, son, and I would venture to say that liars are the worst kind of people in the world. Never lie. No matter what it costs, no matter how much trouble you might get into, or you will end up like Mr. Roy. It's not that Mr. Roy is a bad person, but he did make some really bad decisions today. I want you to learn from mistakes like Mr. Roy's, because I expect you to make better decisions in life than men like him do. Do you understand, son?" His voice was mellow and relaxing like it always was when he was trying to teach The Orphan something new.

"I shouldn't have done to Mr. Roy what I did." The Dad continued. "Today was proof that even adults need to be taught lessons. Mr. Roy needed to be taught a lesson, and I took it upon myself to be the one to teach it to him. Can you tell me what lessons those were today?" The Dad asked in an even tone.

"Well." The Orphan was scratching his head, trying to remember everything that had just happened. "Mr. Roy needed to be taught not to lie because he broke the agreement with me?" The Orphan was trying to search for more to say.

"That's right, son. What about me? I learned something too." The Dad was eager for The Orphan to continue.

The Orphan didn't disappoint.

"I don't know, Dad. You always tell me that you know everything, so what did you need to be taught?" The Orphan said it with such seriousness that The Dad burst out into his familiar, hoarse laugh.

"Don't you ever forget it, son! I do know everything, but that doesn't mean I don't need to be reminded of certain things sometimes."

The Orphan could tell the question caught The Dad off-guard, in a good way.

"You see, Mr. Roy is going to hire you again. You will make more money off him, not because I went over there and collected the money, and not because he is scared that I will visit him again if he doesn't pay. He invited you back because of you!

"You never got angry or lost your temper, and you didn't let your personal feelings get in the way of doing business with him. I may have collected the money but you, son, YOU, made that man realize what a great person you are— and because of that, he will be a customer for life!" The Dad was more than proud. He was amazed at the level of communication and interpersonal skills his son actually had.

"Mr. Roy was certainly right about one thing. You are a different boy, and I am proud to have you as my son.

The Orphan almost burst into tears, right there on the spot.

He had never had someone say they were proud of him, much less proud that he was a part of their family.

The Orphan stood up, took a few steps toward his dad, and gave him a hug. Something that he rarely did on his own accord—for anyone.

For the rest of the day, The Orphan forgot about his bad school year and about what had happened with Dustin. He was so caught up in The Dad being proud and sticking up for him that nothing else mattered.

That was the day The Orphan no longer thought of The Dad as "The Dad."

He thought of him as just, "Dad."

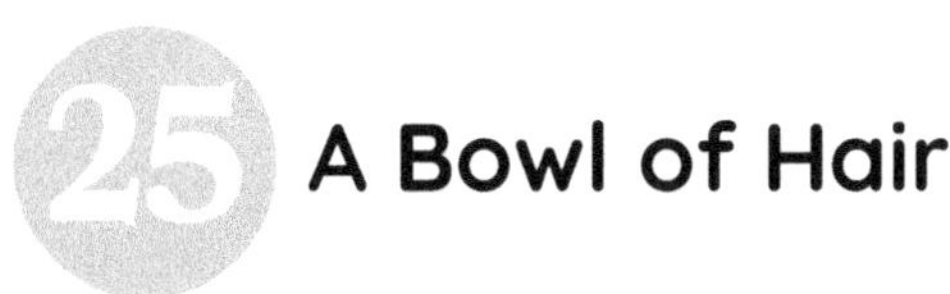

A Bowl of Hair

The Orphan hated his weekly haircuts. It was the same every week.

On Sunday after church, The Mom would take out the shears, go outside, and give the dog's fur a trim. She would wash the blades, shampoo them, and then make sure they were clean before she turned her attention to her son.

After calling his name, she would always patiently wait. She knew she wouldn't have to wait long because if she did, his dad would surely end the delay in a dramatic way.

As she sat there waiting on The Orphan, she would take the time to clean and oil the clippers. She would carefully inspect them for any leftover dog hair. Satisfied that she had cleaned the clippers sufficiently, she would give one more final shout—more of a warning than anything else.

This whole process had started several years ago.

The Mom used to cut his hair before Buffy and Lady's, but his temper tantrums became so intense that The Mom had finally had enough.

"If you don't get your ass on this stool and get your haircut without throwing a fit, I am going to cut the dogs' fur first from now on, since they know how to behave better than you!" She was boiling with frustration.

Just moments before her blow up, The Orphan had insulted The Mom at least six times in twenty seconds, calling her everything from "Mom the Butcher," to "The Scalper," and many more.

His face would always be red and puffy, as if he had just gotten the beating of his life. In reality, it was all a drama show put on by none other than The Orphan himself. It was all designed to get the attention he needed to stop the agonizing task of getting a haircut, or to gain sympathy from those around him.

He would scream, yell, cry, and spit, all before throwing himself around the room. Legs and arms would flail around, hitting the walls and floors as violently as he could without inflicting any true damage to himself.

The first time he did this, it worked. The neighbor's mother came over to check on him, but, upon surveying the scene, quickly made the decision that it was just an act, not actual abuse.

Although they were way over the top, The Orphans' tantrums were not totally unjustified.

It wasn't just the fact that the shears were used on the dogs, it was that the blades were always catching in his hair and ripping out more hair than they trimmed. The sound of the clippers tearing out his hair follicles from their roots made The Orphan not only cringe, but tears would form in the corners of his eyes from the pain.

At that point, his imagination would take over. He could picture chunks of hair being ripped out of his head with blood starting to ooze out of the naked pores. He felt like he was in an old western where the Indian would scalp the Cowboy and hold up his hair in victory!

To be fair, it wasn't The Mom's fault.

The Orphan's hair was so thick that even the professional razors at the barber shop would rip the hair out of his head. The Orphan would make such a scene in public that his dad and The Mom had decided just to do the haircuts themselves at home.

The Orphan sat there in his room, replaying that day over and over in his head, before the recognizable shrill of the "last call" interrupted his train of thought.

The Orphan submitted himself, walking down the stairs to sit on the stupid stool of doom, and serve his penance.

God had a simple but effective way of punishing his children.

That's how he looked at it, anyways. These haircuts were God's way of punishing him for all the sins he had committed over the past week. The amount of pain reflected the severity of the sin.

There was no other explanation as to why God would give him so much hair that it had to be cut once a week. It was silly. None of the other kids got haircuts that often, and none of them had stories of their hair being ripped out by the roots.

He reached the kitchen bar after "the walk of shame," which consisted of marching down the hallway, past his gloating sisters' rooms, and down to The Mom who always tried to put on a happy show when he turned the corner.

He hated the looks The Sisters gave him every week as he passed their doorways. It was almost as if the pain he went through was bringing them enjoyment as well.

It probably did.

Before sitting on the stool, he gave The Mom one last pathetic look, hoping for mercy. Upon seeing that he would receive none, he plopped down on the stool and awaited his torture.

The Mom only had to reach for the clippers before The Orphan's eyes started watering. Before he could serenade everyone with his whining and whimpering, his dad's voice broke out.

"Quit being such a titty baby, son!" his dad called from the living room, where he took his afternoon nap every Sunday.

He took the phrase "titty baby" from Grandpa.

The Orphan was quick to respond.

"Have you ever had your hair ripped out by this stupid thing?! Oh, that's right. You don't get haircuts... because you don't have any hair!" The Orphan replied with more irritation and anger in his voice than he had intended.

The Mom giggled quietly under her breath, as if afraid his dad would hear.

The Orphan could hear the familiar sounds of his dad getting up from the couch with difficulty.

"That's right. I HAVE lost all my hair!" he exclaimed in a booming but playful voice.

His dad was on his feet, walking into the kitchen, toward the bar stool where The Orphan was sitting.

Normally, The Orphan would have been scared to have an adult approach him, but his dad was different.

His dad didn't get angry, as long as you didn't break the rules. He didn't punch or slap when he disciplined him and, most of all, he protected The Orphan's body; he never hurt it.

It had been a long time since someone had hit or used his body for anything...

The Tabernacky Family had never done the things to him the other places before them had. He wanted to tell them how much he loved them for it, how they had saved him, and how they made him safe, but if he told them those things, they would ask questions, questions he could not answer because it would mean breaking "The Promise."

That was something that he just couldn't do. Ever!

Better to keep things the same.

His dad's voice broke out again, interrupting his train of thought.

"That's because I gave all my hair to you!" He had a half grin on his face and was almost at the stool where The Orphan was seated.

The look on his dad's face let The Orphan know exactly what he was about to do.

"No, Dad. Don't!" The Orphan broke out into a huge smile and braced himself for what was about to happen.

The Mom turned off the clippers and took a couple steps back so she could let her husband and son roughhouse a little.

Before The Orphan could block the incoming hand, it was attached to his knee cap. His dad always clawed his hands up like a hawk and went straight for the kneecaps.

"Maybe since you have taken my hair, I can take your knees!" he forced out between clenched teeth as he continued to tickle his son.

Sometimes his dad would grab onto his knees so tightly that The Orphan's laugh would turn into cries for mercy; his dad's fingers dug into his knees so deeply. No matter how much it hurt, however, he would never ask his dad to stop.

As much as it hurt, he liked it. Not only did it make him feel like he was actually a part of a family, but he also knew it was his dad's way of bonding with him.

"Look at this hair, Mom," his dad declared.

It was a house rule to call The Mom, "Mom." It was a rule that even his dad followed.

As a matter of fact, he didn't even remember what The Mom's real name was. All he knew was that she was Mom.

Something clicked inside The Orphan's head.

He was no longer paying attention to what his dad was saying as his mind wandered.

He didn't think of his mom as "The Mom" anymore. A small smile came to his face as his dad's words continued to land on deaf ears.

For The Orphan, it was a startling revelation.

He remembered the day "The Dad" became just Dad.

It had been a couple years ago when he had just started his pooper-scooper business.

That day, The Orphan discovered what it felt like to have someone believe him, stick up for him, and be proud of him. It was a defining moment in his life that he had played over and over in his head as a constant reminder of what other kids must feel when their real parents are proud of them.

He had been waiting a long time to think of "The Mom," as just Mom, but until this moment, for whatever reason, he never had.

It was a riddle he didn't have much time to try and solve due to his dad's persistent teasing.

"Have you ever seen a boy with so much hair? If I knew having a son meant losing my hair so he could have more than he needs, I might have opted for another daughter instead." He repeated again, apparently catching on that his son was daydreaming again.

He was looking down at The Orphan with a smile on his face, making sure that the joke was taken with the warm-heartedness that he intended.

The Orphan didn't skip a beat.

"No, you wouldn't! You're tired of having a house full of girls. You need me just so you don't go... INSANE!" The Orphan was pleased with his comeback.

His dad was done tickling him, so he sat down on the stool next to The Orphan and rubbed his knees.

His dad always had to rub his knees, and sometimes he would even have to ask The Orphan to do it for him. Each year that passed, The Orphan could see that his dad's battle wounds were starting to take their toll on him.

"You are too smart for your own good. When you're right, you're right, though. I need another man in the house. I would settle for Buffy, but sometimes he's as moody as a woman...." He let the words hang in the air as if he was waiting for something.

He didn't have to wait long. His mom was the first one to respond.

"Watch it. You two are outnumbered, outsmarted, and outclassed," Mom replied, only half in jest.

Mom was in full feminist mode.

"Don't undermine the man of the house, but never let a sexist comment go unchallenged." That's what Bridget said she had learned from their mom a long time ago. The Orphan did not understand all this "feminist" stuff, but one thing he did know was that both The Sister Bridget and Mom took it very seriously. When The Orphan talked to his sister Valerie about it, she always told him that she thought it was stupid.

"Men and women can't do the same things, brother. Our bodies, minds, and ways of doing things are different for a reason. If we could just learn to do those things together, I think this world would be a better place."

Having so many points of view in one household used to confuse The Orphan, but it didn't take him long to figure out how he could use it to his benefit during an argument, or something as simple as getting what he wanted.

Of course, his dad knew all this about the women in his household; he was just having a little fun at their expense.

Anytime The Orphan or his dad would say anything derogatory about any woman, Bridget would chalk it up as male chauvinist behavior.

His dad was the farthest thing from a male chauvinist there was. He never yelled at The Mom, always opened her doors, and he loved her unlike anyone The Orphan had ever seen love another person on earth.

The screen door opened and slammed shut.

The Orphan could hear the annoying sound of flip flops headed their way.

"He's like a mutant. Isn't he, Dad? Except instead of superpowers, he has super hair!" Valerie joked, as she came walking into the kitchen in her normal summer attire, consisting of a hot colored tank top, denim shorts, and flip flops.

Valerie always showed up around his haircut time.

A loud thudding noise, followed by the familiar stomping of someone headed down the stairs, let The Orphan know that Bridget was headed down the stairs to join in the fray.

"Hey, Michael, how does it feel to know the dogs get their hair cut first?" Her voice had the same mocking tone as it always did when she was being playful with him.

"Look! You have dog hair mixed in with yours. You are looking more like the dog, you are—every day!" Bridget was looking at him with mischief in her eyes.

The Orphan knew what this was.

Bridget was what she called "The Next Generation of Women," the generation of women who will stand up for women's rights, fight for equality, and unlike Mom, assert Female Dominance while diminishing Male Dominance.

The Orphan didn't understand what all that meant. What he did understand was what got under her skin quicker than anything else.

"Aren't you supposed to be barefoot and doing dishes somewhere, WOMAN?" The Orphan shot back.

The sexist comment had the desired effect.

"You little shit." Bridget's face turned red instantly as she grabbed a shoe off her foot and was poised to throw it at him.

"Bridget!!" their dad's voice snapped.

Bridget came to her senses immediately. Everyone knew not to test their dad.

No one needed a reminder of how quickly that belt could come off.

"GOD! That little twerp gets away with everything! You just wait until Mom and Dad aren't here to save you. I'm going to get you back, you little dweeb."

"That's enough!" Their dad was on his feet. Now it was his face that was getting red, and his hand was hovering around his belt line, sending the message that he was getting ready to whip off his belt and slap it across her ass with the next remark she made.

It was like a scene from an old western where two cowboys squared off, ready to see who would draw first.

Bridget broke her gaze from their dad and just glared at her little brother in silent hatred. She knew what he was doing. She knew her little brother was a pro at playing people against each other.

If she tried to make fun of him, she got into trouble. If she tried to tell on him for something, she would get a guilt trip from The Orphan that would prevent her from betraying him.

The Orphan gave her a careful smirk, making sure no one could see him.

"You won this time, you little jerk, but remember payback is a..."

"Bridget! Go to your room right now!" The Mom had the clippers in her hand and was pointing to the stairs with squinted eyes and pursed lips.

"Fine, but don't blame me when he grows up to be a little delinquent! He always gets what he wants. It's not fair!" Bridget stomped up the stairs in a fit of rage and the look that she shot him could have melted dry ice.

The Orphan looked at Valerie and smiled at her as soon as Bridget disappeared up the hallway. She smiled back in understanding and agreement.

Valerie enjoyed the show as much as he enjoyed putting it on.

The victory was short-lived as The Orphan heard the ominous sound of the clippers coming back on—indicating Mom was ready to resume the haircut.

Stroke after stroke, the clipper blades would get caught in his hair, pulling out a chunk, and with each one of those strokes, The

Orphan was forced to hold his tongue and wince because his dad sat next to him, making sure he wasn't being a "Titty Baby."

After what seemed like hours, the clippers stopped buzzing, and his mom put them back in the box they had come from. She pulled out the scissors next and started to go to work on his bangs and around the edges of his ears.

"You haven't been cleaning your ears, son," she commented in a motherly tone. "Do I need to come in during bath time? Do it for you like I would a little baby?" Her voice was not bitter or even condescending.

She was sending a clear message, and he read it loud and clear.

"NO, MOM! NO! Girls are not allowed in the bathroom during boy bath time," he cried out in disgust.

The Orphan was adamant about this rule. He had set it in place a couple years ago, and he didn't want to have it changed because of a little dirt behind the ears.

"Well, if I am going to treat you like a big boy, then you are going to have to act like one. Wash your ears and clean your cracks," she warned him.

I hate that saying.

"I will." He said half -heartedly. He would try but, in the end, he knew things would probably stay the same. He didn't have time to worry about stupid things like baths, ears, and cracks. There was more to life than rules.

Mom would take care of him, and he knew it, so he didn't worry about her rebukes too much.

The Orphan actually loved the way Mom disciplined him. She had only gotten angry with him once that he could remember, and that was his fault. She was always patient and never really gave him direct orders like his dad did. She used suggestions and stories to get her point across, instead of orders and commands.

This was in direct contrast to the swift, and sometimes violent, discipline he received from his dad.

As much as The Orphan hated his haircuts, he knew that his mom loved giving them to him.

Of course, they could afford to take him to get haircuts if they wanted to but like family dinners, this time together had become a bonding moment for his parents.

"All done," Mom stated without warning.

The Orphan waited for her to brush off the hair clippings, remove the apron, and dust some baby powder on his neck to help prevent irritation.

As soon as she gave him the reassuring pat on the back he was waiting for, The Orphan bolted out the back screen door to play outside in the hot, summer sun.

 # Making Amends

Later that night, as they sat at the dinner table, his sister Bridget wouldn't even look at him.

He didn't know why, but he started to feel bad for his behavior toward her earlier that day.

The whole meal he kept trying to crack jokes and goof around to get her to break her somber mood, but she showed no signs of giving in.

Crap. I am going to have to apologize to her.

He didn't know why he needed to apologize to her, but something in his gut told him it was important.

Even if you think you're right, it's important to apologize.

That thought kept repeating itself over and over in his head, getting louder and louder all the way through dinner and family time.

Finally, thirty minutes before it was lights out, he opened his door and took the few short steps across the hall to Bridget's bedroom door.

With a final deep breath, he raised his hand, knocked on the door, and waited for the sound of her footsteps to confirm she was going to let him in.

Nothing.

He knocked one more time.

Nothing.

She wasn't going to make this easy.

"Bridget. I have something to say to you," The Orphan confessed without trying to show any desperation in his voice.

Again, nothing.

"Fine. If you won't let me in, I will talk to your door!" He waited.

Nothing.

He continued.

"I'm sorry for what I did earlier today. I didn't mean to make you mad. Will you please forgive me?" There was desperation in his voice now.

The silence was killing him.

Soon, The Orphan's desperation started to turn into anger.

The Bible told him that if he asked for forgiveness, SHE was supposed to give it to him.

"Fine, you can be mad at me all you want, but I still love you, and I am still going to try and make you laugh and love me, no matter how much you hate me!" The Orphan spewed.

He turned, walked away, and had almost closed the door to his room when he heard footsteps coming from Bridget's room.

Relief washed over The Orphan as he realized that his last-ditch effort to get Bridget to respond... had worked! But when she opened the door, he did not get the greeting he was expecting.

"Do you know how many times I stick up for you?" Her eyes were bloodshot, and her face was puffy from crying.

"I know. I'm sorry," The Orphan responded without hesitation.

If he had one weakness, it was seeing someone he cared about crying. He had no defenses to protect himself against a vulnerable person, because in the foster homes he grew up in, HE was always the vulnerable person.

She looked at her little brother with suspicion.

"Please, Bridget, I don't want you to be mad at me," The Orphan pleaded. He was being sincere for a change.

Seeing her hesitate gave him the confidence to continue.

"I don't know why I do the things I do. They make me feel good at first, but then I feel bad for doing them later. I know you love me, and you protect me, and I want you to forgive me. Please?"

The Orphan was now crying, in a rare display of remorse.

"You are an evil little boy. You know that? I can't stay mad at you. No one can! That's why you always get what you want. I forgive you, even though I KNOW you will do it again. Now stay out of my room so I can finish being mad at you... alone." With that, she closed the door, and he could hear her walk back to her bed and lay down.

The waterbed she slept on made the swishing noise it always did when someone laid down on it. The Orphan took a deep breath as he realized that although he may have pushed Bridget too far, she still loved him.

To him, that's all that mattered.

Satisfied with himself, The Orphan closed his door and laid down on his bed. He reached inside his pillowcase and pulled out the familiar M&M's packet that he always stuffed in there for a midnight snack. He popped a couple in his mouth and said a quick prayer. He thanked the Lord for everything that He had done for The Orphan that day—for allowing Bridget to forgive him, and asked if the Lord would help him not hurt people's feelings the next day—and every day thereafter.

After the prayer, he lay there remembering the time he had made fun of her body, and he had made a promise to never say mean or bad things about a woman's body, no matter their outward appearance.

He had kept that promise and Bridget had kept hers, but this feminist binge that Bridget was on really started to get confusing as to what she really wanted.

How could a woman be angry about being a woman? What kind of equality is she fighting for? Why would a woman WANT to do what a man does?

Eventually The Orphan got tired of asking questions that he did not know the answer to.

"Control what you can—and give the rest to God." His dad's advice came echoing into his mind.

It was Bridget who came to tuck The Orphan in that night, but he was already sound asleep when she went to kiss him goodnight.

Upon seeing her little brother peacefully sleeping, she realized that she had not only forgiven him this time, but she always would. After all, who else was going to protect him from himself?

With that final thought, she walked over to The Orphan's bedside, gave him a kiss on the forehead, turned off his night light, and gently closed his door behind her.

 # The Runaway

The Orphan trotted down the makeshift trail with the late afternoon sun beaming down on his face as he grinned from ear to ear.

The Notch was a hole in the school playground fence that was located in the dense trees and bushes at the back of the property where the teachers did not patrol.

It was a hot spot for ditchers and smokers. It seemed weird to The Orphan that kids in elementary school smoked and ditched. Valerie would ditch school and smoke, but she was in junior high where they didn't have recess, get to read books with pictures, or have nap time. Junior high sounded so boring. He was sure that he was going to ditch when he got there too.

The Notch provided perfect cover for anyone hiding out there, due to the weeds and vines that had grown all through the chain-link fence, making it impossible to see through to the other side.

Today, The Orphan intended on using The Notch for a different purpose.

He couldn't have picked a better day to run away from home.

All that talk about how cold it was this winter seemed silly with the warm air entering his lungs, filling him with new life at each breath. Sparrows chirped playfully in the Russian olive trees that littered the landscape behind the school playground.

Dad had always told him, "A man is closer to God out in the wilderness."

So, if Jesus was closer to God in the wilderness, maybe he would be too. After all, he was not totally convinced there was a God, so this adventure seemed like a good time for a burning bush to pop up and prove to The Orphan that He truly did exist.

A pang of homesickness started to creep in.

The Orphan was going to miss his arrowhead hunting, antler searching, and Native American jewelry searches that he always took with his dad and his dad's friend Bob.

The snow that had fallen earlier that week had melted into the clay-like sand that stuck to the bottom of his shoes. It was soft and he liked how his feet sunk into the earth. He suddenly wished he was walking barefoot with mud squeezing in between his toes.

Whenever he said things like this to The Dad, he would always shake his head with a grin on his face and mumble, "Hippie," under his breath.

The Orphan liked walking in the mud, he thought, resisting the urge to take his shoes and socks off.

This drove The General nuts because in the military, the only thing you took better care of than your rifle was your feet.

The reasons were simple.

In war time, soldiers would get their feet cut, infection would set in, and in some cases, this would even kill the soldier.

The most graphic example The General gave were the pongee traps the Vietcong would set.

First, they would dig a two-and-a-half- to three-foot hole. Next, they would make wooden spikes, stick them into the ground, and fill the hole with animal feces and human remains. Once they had filled the hole up three quarters of the way with the infectious concoction, they would carefully cover the trap for the unsuspecting enemy soldier to step into.

Once soldiers' legs were penetrated by the wooden stakes, the infectious material would enter into their bloodstream. In some cases, the wounds would never heal, always oozing a green, infectious pus out of the original puncture wounds.

A shiver went down The Orphan's spine as he instinctively started searching the ground for pongee traps. It was silly. This wasn't Vietnam, but it helped him stay focused on what he was doing and away from what he was leaving behind.

If it could happen to a battle-hardened soldier, then it sure could happen to a ten-year-old like me as well.

With this thought, The Orphan put aside his impulse to go all-natural and sided with caution, opting to leave his shoes and socks on.

If he was going to live on his own, he was going to have to remember all the survival skills his dad had showed him, the cooking skills his mom had taught him, and the social skills that Valerie and Bridget had pointed out throughout the years.

He was going to miss everyone, but he hadn't really been given a choice.

As soon as The General received the phone call from Mrs. Williams that his grades had dropped to mostly Ds and Fs, he was going to get the beating of his life!

To his mom and dad, education was almost as important as breathing! Getting Ds and Fs in school was a slap in the face to both of them.

He remembered the time he was getting a bad grade in kindergarten for his handwriting. For three months, he had to come home and practice his alphabet penmanship for an hour and half each day, including the weekends!

Then there was the time his teachers had let his parents know that he was below the reading level for his age group.

They had hired a tutor for six months to make sure that he was not only at his grade level, but above the next two grade levels as well!

It was like school with overtime, without overtime pay, or any benefits for that matter.

If child labor laws existed to prevent him from working too many hours as a child, then there should be laws put in place to make sure that he didn't spend too much time on education as well.

That's how he thought of it, anyway.

Today's report card was going to have nuclear consequences, and he didn't want to be there to find out what they were. A lot of time, sweat, and money had gone into his education.

As an Orphan, he was already at a disadvantage emotionally and physically, and the fight to keep him passing to the next grade was a never-ending task for his parents.

For years, he had been testing the limits with his mom and dad, but this would be the final straw that sent him back to the Orphanage.

He was sure of it.

Running away would stop that. If he ran away, then there would be no way to take him back. If they didn't take him back, then he still had a family, even if he was in exile.

From where he stood, disowned was better than re-gifted.

As he walked along the beaten-down path of a game trail toward his destination, his mind wandered to his family and what they would be doing right now.

The General would be building a fire in the fireplace, the smell of burning wood along with orange embers glowing in the dim den room. Mom would be starting the preparations for her nightly home-cooked meal.

Not to mention, it was *Disney Masterpiece Theatre* night, which meant Mom's famous brownies were being baked as well.

There were so many things he was going to miss. He was starting to wish he hadn't screwed things up and pushed them so far. They were a good family, and all of them wanted the best for him. The fact that he acted out so much wasn't their fault, but he continued to make them pay the price for it.

Maybe it was better for everyone that he was leaving, not just him.

A chill went up The Orphan's spine.

 **Shiprock**

The Orphan was thankful that he had remembered to wear his leather pilot flight jacket as he wrapped it tighter across his body. It was definitely starting to cool down as the West sun disappeared behind "The Shiprock."

The Shiprock was still his favorite natural structure. It stood for everything that embodied who he was, who he wanted to be, and it continued to remind him that it was okay to be alone in this world.

In more ways than one, it proved to be a compass for him, always pointing him in whatever direction would help him get over any life hurdles that were being put in front of him.

The Orphan noticed that it was starting to quickly get dark.

I'd better find some shelter if I am going to keep from getting sick.

The thought marched into his head without warning.

Once he got to his destination, he would try to find some chicken noodle soup, pop it into the microwave, and find a place to bed down. The only other thing that could be better was if he were to find some hot chocolate packets as well.

There was nothing better than a bowl of chicken noodle soup for dinner and a cup of hot chocolate before you go to bed. The thought of the delicious fluid warming him up from the inside out gave him new energy.

The Orphan was startled, as he heard a branch break off in the distance behind him. His body froze instantly, as his imagination started to race.

He remembered how The General told him that Bollack allowed bears and mountain lions on his property, offering them a sanctuary from hunters and poachers. Trappers and hunters would bring cubs from the targets they had hunted that season, dropping them off so his sanctuary would take care of them.

Suddenly, The Orphan felt vulnerable, like he was being hunted.

He started to run as the possibilities took hold of him, feeding a fear that seized control of his mind and body.

He zigged and zagged through the trees, refusing to look back at what could be pursuing him. His lungs felt like they were getting ready to burst! It was cold, and sweat was starting to form all over his body.

As he broke through the next group of trees, The Orphan found himself in the middle of an old dirt road. As he looked to his left, he could see that it led all the way back down the Bollack property to a paved road that connected to the main highway, about two miles up the road. When he looked to his right, he couldn't believe his luck.

Across the bridge and a few hundred yards up the dirt road was his destination.

The Orphan remained completely silent for several minutes, making sure no vehicles were traveling up the road. If anyone spotted him, they would turn him back over to his parents.

A smile came to his face as he realized that not only was he in no danger from some wild animal chasing him, but that he was actually ahead of his estimated arrival time. He thought it would be at least a couple hours after dark before he got there, and now it only seemed that he was thirty minutes or so away.

This would give him more time to explore and find a good hiding place for a few weeks before he could find a way to skip town.

Satisfied that no one was coming, he headed up the road toward the bridge.

# Old Friends

Dad was a great woodsman and would always show The Orphan how the position of the sun could give an estimate of the time, the moss on the rocks could give the direction you were headed, and the current of the water could always help you find civilization.

The Orphan looked west, toward the departing sun, and decided that he had about an hour and a half before sundown.

Plenty of time to scope everything out and get settled in.

As he started to walk, he realized that his feet were making a squishing sound, confirming his socks and shoes had gotten wet in the damp underbrush.

"Crap." He should have packed a few extra pairs of socks, in case this happened. His mind wandered again to something his dad would always tell him about wet feet.

In the war, men had to take care of their feet, so they didn't get "Swamp Feet," which was a nasty condition that soldiers got when they walked long distances with wet feet in the jungles of Vietnam.

Although it was not fatal in itself, if a person incurred an open wound on their foot during battle or even during the march, the wound could contract gangrene, which could prove fatal.

He would find a place to make a fire, hang up his socks on a stick over the fire like The General had taught him during camping, dry his feet, and he would be fine.

The thought never occurred to him that he had no fire-starting paraphernalia; not only that, but he lacked the skills to build one anyway.

With the sun going down and the cold setting in, The Orphan started to realize how hungry he was.

Mom probably had dinner on the table, and they would all be eating by now. Mom's cooking was always so good, and every time Dad talked to The Orphan about finding a good woman, he would always ask:

"Son, do you know what the key to man's heart is?"

"No," The Orphan always responded, even though he already knew the answer.

"His stomach, son. His stomach is the key to his heart, son. If you find a woman that can cook, you keep her because your stomach is one of the VERY few things that doesn't stop working as you get older." He would always chuckle at the end of that comment, as if he was laughing at some inside joke.

Maybe he was. After all, no matter how many times The Orphan had heard the inside joke, he still didn't know what it meant. Every time he tried to ask; all he would get for an answer was:

"Some things you just need to learn as you get older. Believe me, this is one of them."

The memory faded as The Orphan noticed the sun was sinking faster than he anticipated.

I had better hurry, or I won't have time to eat and set up camp, he thought as he started to pick up the pace.

Before he made the final stretch to his destination, his mind wandered back to how much he was going to miss his family.

He hadn't told anyone he was leaving, including Valerie. He was going to miss her, and she would probably wonder why he hadn't told her what he was planning. After all, she had always shared with him her plans to do the same, and one day, she even told him of her plan to kill herself.

That thought hung in his mind, taunting him.

"I am going to slit my wrists and bleed out like they do in the movies, Mikey. No one cares about me anymore anyway so why not?"

"I care about you. If you leave me, then who will be my friend? No one else will be my friend because I don't have a real mom or dad, and they think that is weird. No one will be your friend because of your diabetes, and they think that is weird. We were meant to be friends. You can't kill yourself. I need you, Valerie. Don't leave me."

The Orphan was not crying the night he spoke those words to Valerie, but he was crying as he turned the bend and came upon the Bollack house.

And now, I have left her by herself.

The thought hit him like a ton of bricks, but it was too late.

He had made up his mind, and he was already at the first part of his destination. The next thing he would do is hitchhike to Albuquerque. He would then find a way to be reunited with his "REAL FAMILY."

He chose Albuquerque because that is where his mom and dad said they picked him up when they adopted him.

Maybe his "real" parents would forgive him for whatever he had done to make them give him away, and they would take him back. If not, he would find another way to survive.

He always did.

His family was better off without him anyway. They always yelled at him and told him that he was always getting into trouble, causing the hair on his dad's head to fall off, and on and on.

Who would want a son or brother like that for long? The tears were flowing uncontrollably now, as he realized how much he was going to miss all of them.

30 The Empty Mansion

A cold breeze forced the memory to the back of his mind as the full chill of the night air hit his wet cheeks.

The Orphan started to panic as he realized how dark it was.

He might have miscalculated how far the mansion was, and how long it would take to find something to eat and make camp.

When The Orphan reached the home driveway, he found the house was empty. For whatever reason, the story of "Goldilocks and the Three Bears" came to mind, and it brought a small smile to his lips.

He strode into the Bollack mansion as if it were his own home.

The Orphan walked through the screen door to the rear entrance of the house and noticed all sorts of rocks and crystals thrown onto benches and old chairs.

There were animal skins, heads with antlers on them, and carved wooden furniture all over the house entrance, followed quickly by the smell of freshly cut and lacquered timber. It reminded him of all the times his dad had let him help build things around the house with his power tools.

He walked through another door, but this time, it was solid wood with carvings of some sort engraved into it.

As soon as his eyes adjusted to the dim light, his heart sank.

The room had more than ten small TVs stacked on top of each other! They were black and white screens and although turned on, nothing seemed to be playing on them.

Upon closer observation, he started to realize what he was looking at.

Displayed on the screen was a whole bunch of trees and wildlife. It was like he had ten channels of the Discovery network on, all at once. It almost looked like a puzzle that had been put together, with each screen picking up where the other one left off.

He had never seen this kind of technology, not even in the cartoons and movies he watched.

Which was A LOT!

Then, something at the bottom of the screen caught his attention.

31 Follow Your North Star

A truck started to cross several of the screens, as if it were passing through each camera in perfect order. It seemed so realistic, like this footage was shooting... right now?!

He looked a little closer at the vehicle, and in moments, he recognized the symbol painted on the old Chevy was "B," for Bollack.

"NO! IT CAN'T BE!" The Orphan could barely force out of his mouth as he stared wide eyed at the screens.

His heart sank as an overwhelming sense of fear and confusion swept over his now-shaking body.

In that instant, The Orphan panicked.

He dropped everything he was holding and ran out the back door, across the cleared area, and into the bushes and trees. He darted past the brush and kept on running, fear driving his every movement.

As he ran, the stories of all the bears and cougars that lived in these forests started to rush into the front of his consciousness as his imagination started to constantly play tricks on him.

Paranoia set in, as every sound and shadow became his enemy.

He stopped to gather his bearings.

The Orphan was bent over, holding his breath, trying to listen to see if anyone was in actual pursuit, when he finally came to his senses and realized he better get serious about his situation.

Taking a deep breath, trying to inject as much oxygen into his lungs and muscles as he could, he finally was able to steady his breathing.

Another thing I learned from my dad, he thought quickly.

Once he finished calming himself down, he realized that it was not only completely dark, but he had no idea in what direction he had run and where he was.

He was completely lost!

More of his dad's training kicked in:

"When faced with fear and panic, a person can only prevail by being calm, determined, and confident of their ability to solve the problem that is in front of them." It was almost like his dad's shadow was there, directing his every thought.

A sense of determination overtook The Orphan.

He started to look for clues that would not only give him his bearing on direction but give him a clue as to where he had ended up in his moment of mindless panic.

The mansion was south of the road, so I need to go north to get back to it.

It didn't matter which way or how far he had run, all that mattered was he needed to go north to the main road.

He looked up into the cloudless night and searched for the North Star. He could see his breath form in front of his eyes with each exhale, and his clothes were starting to get stiff from his sweat freezing into the fabric. He searched and searched as best he could, but the density of the trees prevented him from finding the moon, much less the North Star.

He gave up and tried to think of another way to gain his bearings.

It was too dark to look for landmarks, so he dropped to his knees and started to crawl on the ground, recalling one of his dad's favorite outdoor lessons.

He realized the ground was freezing, so the temperature had to be below freezing.

I had better get to that road and get home or I could freeze to death!

There was so much conviction in the thought that The Orphan forgot all about running away and the trouble he was going to be in over his grades.

His dad may spank him every day for a year for having bad grades, but that was better than freezing to death.

Besides, maybe Bridget would feel sorry for him and save him from his dad's wrath.

The Orphan forced out all other thoughts but survival from his mind.

He crawled all over, hands outstretched, grasping until he finally found what he was looking for.

The stone that he found was large. He couldn't see it, but it had to be half his size. Its texture was not smooth, but rather jagged and coarse.

His heart leapt as the advice his dad had given him rang true:

"Son, if you find yourself lost without the stars or landmarks to guide you, there is always one way that you can find your way." The General's hand had been gently wrapped around the back of his neck, like he enjoyed so much.

"Now close your eyes, and do what I say." His dad's voice had an almost hypnotic tone to it.

The Orphan closed his eyes and waited for his dad's voice command.

"Slowly bend down until you feel your hands hit the dirt."

His dad waited until The Orphan completed the task.

"Now stretch your hands out and secure your body weight."

Again. There was silence until the order was fulfilled.

"Now lower yourself onto your knees and slowly start to crawl until you find a big rock. Make sure the rock is so big, there is no way a single man could pick it up." His voice broke the silence as he saw his son start to scramble, looking for the rock impatiently. *"Move slowly, because you don't want to hurt yourself looking for the rock."*

The Orphan did as he was instructed and, before long, he had found what he was looking for.

Once he had gotten as close to the rock as he could, he waited for his dad to give him further instructions.

"Slowly hover your hand above the rock, just above the surface, until you feel the texture go from hard and rough, to soft and fuzzy."

It took a few seconds, and he had to cautiously move to different sides of the rock. Making the task more difficult was the fact that his dad still had him searching on his knees with his eyes closed.

After a few more moments, he found what he was looking for.

"You can open your eyes now, son." The General proclaimed in a proud voice.

"Moss?" The Orphan had inquired in a quizzical tone.

The General didn't hesitate.

"Moss can grow all over the rock, but nature gives us a clue on how to navigate with this simple trick… As you slide your hand across the top of the rock, you can tell where the moss is the healthiest and thickest. You see, moss is a cool-weather plant, and because of that, the healthiest part of the moss will grow on the north side, in the area your hand feels. It is on the north because it never has the sun, or UV rays, shine directly on it. Find this part of the rock, and you will find North." The General just stood over The Orphan until he saw confirmation that his point had been received.

"That's a really cool trick! Thanks, Dad!" The Orphan had shot back at his father...

The memory brought warmth to The Orphan, despite the freezing temperature. In spite of his declining circumstances, The Orphan was optimistic that he was on the right path once again.

Soon after that, he quickly found the softest part of the moss on the rock, stood up, and started to walk slowly in that direction.

The Orphan's eyes were starting to adjust to the dark, and land-marks started to take shape.

He was glad that he had found his direction, but his feet were starting to hurt. They felt as if they had been put through a cheese grater and then lit on fire! The thought kept morphing into other frightening thoughts with each passing step.

Then he remembered.

Swamp Feet. How long had his feet been wet?

"Swamp Feet" happens when your feet have been wet long enough to make the skin so soft, you can slice it like a knife into butter. Water will then get under your skin and start to create blisters that will soon pop, the wound will crack from friction, and it will start to bleed. If left untreated, that could lead to infection, and infection could lead to death.

This was his dad's way of pointing out that even the littlest mistakes in the wild could lead to a tragic ending.

The Orphan didn't know how much time had passed since he had left the mansion, but one thing he knew for sure was he was in pain, cold, and ready to lay down and go to sleep.

He walked for what seemed miles. The blisters on his feet hurt so bad, he started to walk with a slight limp, and all the sweat he had generated while running had frozen underneath his clothes, making it impossible to warm up.

The trees in front of him parted, and as he stepped into a cleared field looking into a clear, night sky, The Orphan was able to exhale a deep sigh of relief.

He could see cars driving on the highway.

 Survival

The Orphan had chosen the right direction, and although he was about three miles east of his home, he was almost to a place where he could find help.

He marched on with a renewed spirit and determination in his step.

It only took a few more steps before the air got noticeably cooler, almost as if the temperature had dropped ten degrees in a few short steps.

Something wasn't right as his instincts told him the air temperature shouldn't have dropped as much as it did.

Once he realized the cause, he knew his mistake, and he almost burst into tears.

He had gone too far east while running away from Bollack's house, and now he was standing in front of the Animas River.

The Orphan stood there for a few moments, staring at the icy reflection sprawled out in front of him.

He was shivering to the point that his teeth were chattering, his feet felt like thousands of needles were digging into him, and he was soaked from the inside out.

Who knows how long it would take him to travel all the way around it? And going back the way he had come was out of the question.

I'm going to have to cross the river.

The thought came, suddenly.

"That's suicide," The Orphan mumbled out loud, speaking to himself.

He kept replaying the words over and over in his head, all the while trying to convince himself that it was the worst thing he could possibly do.

"Nope. I'm gunna do it," he declared aloud, as if he was trying to win an argument with a person who did not exist.

Knowing he had no time to lose, The Orphan started kicking the ground, searching for a stick big enough to support his weight.

He was going to have to use the stick to jab into the ice and slowly walk across using the stick to make sure the ice was strong enough to hold his weight. There was no way of knowing if it was going to be strong enough, but it would give him an idea of where to place his footing.

Once he found it, he immediately bent down to pick it up. He tried to bend, break, and even snap it up against a rock, but it withstood all the abuse.

Satisfied with the selected talisman he had chosen, The Orphan took a moment to gather his nerves.

Finally, he was as ready as he was ever going to be. The Orphan carefully put one foot in front of the other, making sure he used the stick to pound into the ice, the tip of his toe to slowly distribute his weight onto the ice, and precariously transferring the rest of his body weight in a slow but steady trek across the river.

He tried not to look down too much, letting his instincts take control of the process and the direction that he chose.

The moon was illuminating the sky, and The Orphan could see everything in front of him. An empty field with a sole house on its property was right in front of him, with the highway so close he could feel his dad's fire warming him up, as if he were already in the house.

Trying not to get overconfident, he focused on the task at hand.

"Survivors... survive." The General's voice echoed.

This was the answer he always gave The Orphan when he asked about killing so many Congmen and saving his co-pilot during the war.

The Orphan was going to use that knowledge tonight to make sure he survived crossing The Animas.

33 Crossing the River

This part of The Animas River was about fifty yards across, and The Orphan had no idea how deep it was, which is what he was scared of the most.

He was coming up to the middle of the river—the trickiest part of the crossing because that's where the ice would be the thinnest, and the most dangerous.

A sense of pride swept over The Orphan as he realized not only how much he had learned from his dad, but how much of it he was actually able to apply without any assistance. It wasn't the time or the place to have this kind of thought, but it was true, nonetheless.

As he drew nearer to the center of the ice, he could hear, and even feel, cracking beneath his feet.

He realized the ice was beginning to buckle under his weight!

Things were not looking good. Despite the situation The Orphan was calm.

If he were to fall through the ice, the river would take him where it wanted, how it wanted. He would be swept under the unbroken ice, and even if there were air pockets under the ice, he would only have about five minutes or so before he would freeze to death.

Panic was slowly setting in, and this time he wasn't mentally strong enough to dismiss it.

He looked down—and wished that he hadn't.

The moonlight was so bright that he could not only see the water running beneath his feet, but he could see how fast it was moving!

There is no way I could live through that current!

Without thinking, he abandoned the idea of using the stick and taking his time to cross and started to run as fast as he could, throwing caution to the wind.

One of his feet broke through the ice and his leg plummeted into the water. Pain shot through his leg as the freezing cold water penetrated through his denim jeans. He screamed as he realized the rest of the ice was breaking around him. Realizing that he still had the walking stick, he stabbed it as hard as he could right in front of him as a last-ditch effort to save himself from going under.

It worked.

The branch broke through the ice, hit the bottom of the river, and held strong. So did the rest of the ice around him.

He gained a little confidence as he realized that here, the river was not deeper than his waist. That confidence was short-lived, as his leg still felt the power of the current.

He pulled himself out of the icy water and planted his foot back onto the ice-bed in front of him. Once he realized he had good footing, he finished crossing in the same way he had started.

In a few short moments, The Orphan was across The Animas without another incident.

"Thank you, God," The Orphan managed to say aloud as he looked up to the sky, dropped to his knees, and prayed, remembering his "burning bush" thought earlier.

"God, I don't know how to follow you, but I will, no matter how hard it gets, no matter what the circumstances. When I didn't have a dad, you became my Father, and every time I should have died, you have saved me. Please help me be a better boy, so I don't get bad grades and make my mom and dad mad at me. I really do want them to keep me."

The Orphan just sat there on his knees after he was done praying. He was exhausted and didn't want to walk anymore. His feet hurt, and he was so cold. Sitting here allowed him to finally rest, and although he was still cold, it seemed like that was starting to go away too.

It just felt good to do nothing.

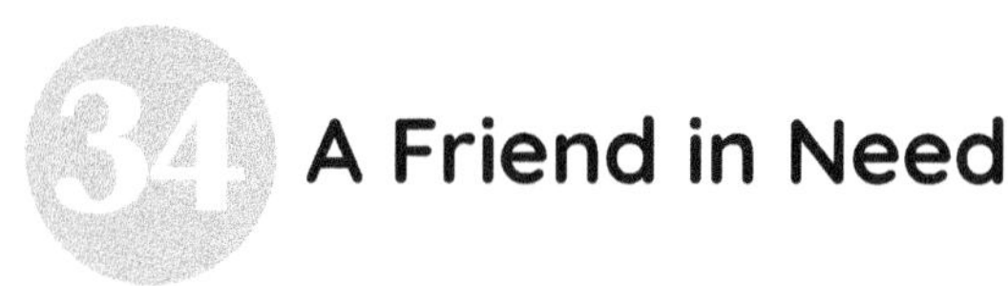

A Friend in Need

"Keep going." It was his dad's shadow speaking to him again, urging him forward.

The Orphan didn't respond.

"Keep going," the shadow repeated.

Finally, The Orphan obeyed.

It took every bit of energy The Orphan had to stand up and start walking across the field. He forced his mind back to the promise that he had made to God, and it kept him going.

It was an easy promise to make, and the more he thought about it, the more he wondered why he had doubted there was a God. Thinking about it now, The Orphan realized that God had been there for him all along.

When he woke up in the hospital with a broken jaw and bruises everywhere, it was God who was telling him he would be safe. When people were beating him or worse, it was God who was instructing him how to survive the blows. The Orphan didn't know how he knew this, but he knew it had to be true.

How else could I still be on this earth? he thought to himself as he trudged through the grassy field.

Once he got to the highway, he realized just how far he had ventured from his home. He was going to have to walk four miles back to his neighborhood.

"You made your bed. Now lay in it." His mom's rebuke popped into his mind.

The Orphan walked with his head down, breathing into his sweat-soaked shirt, trying to get his hot breath to warm him up as he kept on, against traffic toward his home.

When The Orphan looked up, he thought he saw a police squad car headed his way. Its lights were not on, but he thought he could dimly make out the shape of the vehicle.

Hoping his parents had called the police to search for him, The Orphan started to wave his arms, in hopes of flagging the officer down.

As the vehicle got closer, The Orphan realized that it was, in fact, a police cruiser, but it did not even brake as it passed by him.

Flying past The Orphan, the cruiser continued on to its unknown destination.

A couple miles went by, and he saw another police cruiser. This time, he didn't even try to flag it down as it passed by him.

They were probably glad he ran away. They always told him how much trouble he was, and how he had pitted his sisters against each other. Why would they call the police? When he walked through the door, he didn't think they would tell him to leave, but he didn't think that they would be that happy to see him either.

He would find a way to make it up to them. He always did.

That was, if his dad didn't kill him for running away. At least they wouldn't be embarrassed that they had to get a search party assembled for him. If that were the case, then surely someone would have found him by now.

His mind turned away from his home and family and toward his horrible health condition. It really felt like he was going to drop to the ground and die at this point.

He was thirsty, sick, and his feet were in bad shape. The Orphan looked up to make sure he was to the left of the road and not venturing into oncoming traffic. As he looked up, he noticed a vehicle that seemed to be slowing down and headed directly toward him.

As the vehicle moved closer, it slowed all the way to a stop.

It wasn't a police vehicle, his parents van, or any other person that he knew of, so he didn't move any closer. He didn't want to seem eager to enter the vehicle, in case it was a dangerous person.

After all, there was a serial killer in Bloomington, and worse, all the abductions and killings had mostly happened in his neighborhood.

They still hadn't caught the killer, and everyone in Bloomington was on edge.

It was actually a weird story, but The Orphan didn't have time to think of it now, as the door to the vehicle opened.

"Michael! There you are!" A familiar voice rang out.

It was Steven! The Orphan's best friend.

Soon, all the pain and fatigue washed away and was quickly replaced with joy and gratitude.

"Steven! Get your idiot friend and get him in the truck so we can take him home!" Steven's stepdad yelled impatiently.

The Orphan ran to the door with his friend and jumped into the truck, closing the door behind him.

He was met immediately by Trish, Steven's mom.

She wrapped a blanket around The Orphan's shoulders as quickly as she could and started to rub him down to warm him up.

"Are you okay, Michael?" she asked, worried.

Steven's stepdad didn't give him the chance to answer.

"Oh, he's okay now, but when he gets home, and Kent gets ahold of him, then it will be a different story." Steven's step ad was dead serious.

Dave was a very thick man with forearms as big as The Orphan's legs, the squarest jaw of anyone The Orphan knew, and he reminded The Orphan of the Dwarf characters that always carried big axes to war and had short tempers. He had thick black hair and penetrating blue eyes with a voice that boomed with authority.

"He's the kind of man you want on your side in a fight and is loyal to the end," his dad would always say.

In moments, they were pulling into his neighborhood.

Time to pay the piper, The Orphan thought as they pulled up to the curb of his parent's driveway.

In front of the house were two patrol cars and a handful of people standing in the front yard. His dad stood at the front door, looking directly at Steven's stepdad's truck.

Once the truck stopped, The Orphan opened the door and unwrapped the blanket from around his body.

Once he had handed the now-soaked blanket to Trish, The Orphan thanked Dave, and gave Steven one last hug, as if it might be the last time he would see his best friend.

When he turned around to head toward the front door and saw the look on his dad's face, he knew he was going to get it.

This might be the last time I see anyone, he thought as he headed up the red brick pathway to his front door under the cold steady watch of the man he called Dad.

As he looked into his dad's eyes, he knew their relationship would never be the same.

In the military, the penalty for desertion was death, and although they would not actually kill him, that didn't mean they couldn't make his life absolutely miserable.

The Orphan knew change was in the wind, discipline was needed, and his dad, an Army general, was more than capable of carrying his punishment out.

And carry it out, The General would...

Thank you for reading, *An Orphan's Tale*, the first book in the *Hard Knox Chronicles*.

In the sequel, *An Orphan's Tale: The Karate Kids*, The Orphan starts to ask questions and explore his past. In doing so, he finds himself trying to navigate the worst parts of his personality while those around him struggle to keep up with his destructive behavior as revelations of his past emerge.

Meanwhile, new people and personalities enter The Orphan's life that balance out the negative direction he is heading in. Old friends re-emerge and provide support for The Orphan in a small town in which every citizen's secrets are laid bare, for all to see.

Can The Orphan and those around him keep it together as The Law of Unintended Consequences shows the entire butterfly effect of The Orphan from a vulnerable child into a self-destructive, ticking timebomb?

Acknowledgements

First, I would like to thank all six of my children for being who you are, for that has made me who I am.

To my adoptive family, for showing me how a family sticks together.

Suzanne Holman for being a positive influence when I had none.

It takes a community to raise a child so thank you to all the soldiers, officers, teachers and public servants who make this country great.

Last but not least, Jennifer S. Wilkov with Your Book is Your Hook! for coaching, editing, and guiding me to be the best author I can be.

About the Author

B.T Cox writes books about fictional characters who overcome real life odds. 

An Orphan's Tale: Hard Knox Chronicles is the first book in his debut series in which an orphan boy overcomes the challenges of the foster care and adoption process.

He knows the challenges facing those that are unplanned, unwanted and unprepared for and he has spent his lifetime building a roadmap to give a beacon of light to those that have little hope.

Hire Me to Speak at Your Next Meeting or Event

Previous engagements have included orphanages, motivational groups, people with underprivileged environments (battered women's shelters, prison reform organizations, and more), judicial systems, the National Guard, mortgage and realtor associations and more.

Available for interviews upon request.

For more information and to book, go to
https://coloradophoenixproject.org/.

Colorado Phoenix Project

"Every year 4,000 foster children are homeless after they become adult age."
– FinallyFamilyHomes.org

The Colorado Phoenix Project aims to be a leader in assisting our nation's underprivileged youth through our systematic approach and developmental and apprenticeship programs.

For seven years, we have set the foundation to provide:
- Physical fitness and mental wellness programs
- Financial and workforce solution programs
- Awareness and resources for rehabilitation and self-reliance

Professionals from all walks of life have come together to provide the donations needed for our participants to get scholarships for various types of programs.

All proceeds from the sales of this book will be donated to support The Colorado Phoenix Project and its efforts.

As a 501(c)(3) non-profit, your donations help rehabilitative efforts, camaraderie, and community development. By focusing on the mentorship of our youth, we believe The Colorado Phoenix Project and its programs will have a major impact on the communities it serves.

To learn more about The Colorado Phoenix Project,
go to https://coloradophoenixproject.org/.

To make an additional donation, go to
https://bit.ly/Colorado-Phoenix-Project-Donation-Link